Law and Technology

Law and Technology

A Methodical Approach

RYAN CALO

Professor of Law, School of Law and Information School, University of Washington

OXFORD
UNIVERSITY PRESS

OXFORD
UNIVERSITY PRESS

Oxford University Press is a department of the University of Oxford. It furthers the University's objective of excellence in research, scholarship, and education by publishing worldwide. Oxford is a registered trade mark of Oxford University Press in the UK and in certain other countries.

Published in the United States of America by Oxford University Press
198 Madison Avenue, New York, NY 10016, United States of America.

Library of Congress Cataloging-in-Publication Data
Names: Calo, Ryan author
Title: Law and technology : a methodical approach / Ryan Calo.
Description: New York : Oxford University Press, 2025. |
Includes bibliographical references and index.
Identifiers: LCCN 2025035499 (print) | LCCN 2025035500 (ebook) |
ISBN 9780197526132 hardback | ISBN 9780197526163 epub |
ISBN 9780197526170 online | ISBN 9780197526156 updf
Subjects: LCSH: Technology and law
Classification: LCC K487.T4 C35 2025 (print) | LCC K487.T4 (ebook) |
DDC 344/.095—dc23/eng/20250730
LC record available at https://lccn.loc.gov/2025035499
LC ebook record available at https://lccn.loc.gov/2025035500

DOI: 10.1093/9780197526170.001.0001

Printed by Marquis Book Printing, Canada

The manufacturer's authorized representative in the EU for product safety is Oxford University Press España S.A. of Parque Empresarial San Fernando de Henares, Avenida de Castilla, 2 – 28830 Madrid (www.oup.es/en or product.safety@oup.com). OUP España S.A. also acts as importer into Spain of products made by the manufacturer.

Note to Readers

This publication is designed to provide accurate and authoritative information in regard to the subject matter covered. It is based upon sources believed to be accurate and reliable and is intended to be current as of the time it was written. It is sold with the understanding that the publisher is not engaged in rendering legal, accounting, or other professional services. If legal advice or other expert assistance is required, the services of a competent professional person should be sought. Also, to confirm that the information has not been affected or changed by recent developments, traditional legal research techniques should be used, including checking primary sources where appropriate.

(Based on the Declaration of Principles jointly adopted by a Committee of the American Bar Association and a Committee of Publishers and Associations.)

For my father Michael and my mother Mary Ann,
the original Professor Calo.

Contents

INTRODUCTION

Amish communities only adopt technologies that comport with their values of humility and community. When, of necessity, the Amish avail themselves of technology, they frequently choose less recent or convenient forms. Amish furniture-makers may use hydraulic drills, for example, or conduct business only on a public payphone.[1]

Amish teenagers are invited to explore modern technology during a period known as the "rumspringa." The 2002 documentary *Devil's Playground* depicts a young man playing videogames in his room using the electricity from his car running outside.[2] Even so, most Amish teens return to the fold. Meanwhile, in New York City, kids identifying as "neo-Luddites" have begun to reject iPhones in favor of flip phones and film cameras.[3] They get together in parks and read books or draw sketches. Orthodox Jews intensely debate what technologies can be used on the *Shabbat*. "Confronting unfamiliar technologies," writes historian Amy Sue Bix, "observers sought to dissect their physical properties to determine if any component violated *Shabbat* rules."[4] Artifacts and systems that amount to work must be put aside.

Learning about the ways the Amish, neo-Luddites, Orthodox Jews, and others, engage with emerging technology can help break down the reflexive tendency to accept technology on its own terms. These communities ask not how to accommodate everyday artifacts and systems, but when and whether. To wonder how technology can be made to conform to community values, rather than disrupt or displace them, is to swim upstream against the prevailing current of modern Western thought.

Whatever we are acculturated to believe, nothing about the physical and digital artifacts and systems we use every day is inevitable. Technology is ultimately a social fact,[5] its design and use occurring against the backdrop of human rules and norms. Technology can be mandatory or forbidden, and everything in between. It is up to each society and community to dictate what rules it ought to follow. Though it may feel otherwise, there is no legitimate reason to believe technology to be any less governable than marriage,

Law and Technology. Ryan Calo, Oxford University Press. © Ryan Calo 2025.
DOI: 10.1093/9780197526170.003.0001

markets, travel, religion, or any other set of social facts that make up our complicated world.

Technology holds a profound influence over contemporary life. Itself beholden to social and societal forces, technology plays a significant role in establishing our individual and collective affordances, that is, what humans are able to imagine and do. For centuries it made reasonable sense to talk about the ways people accomplished tasks *with* technology. Today, technology is the medium *through* which we do anything—less a tool than an environment. Bruno Latour's adage, that "technology is society made durable,"[6] has never felt truer.

This is a book about technology's intersection with another crucial aspect of contemporary society: the law. Law and policy are among the only formal mechanisms a society has by which to promote, restrain, or channel technology. Law is the domain within which communities negotiate and enforce an important array of rights, limits, and obligations. Technology is a powerful social force. But the people who design, build, disseminate, and use technology remain nevertheless subject to the law. To read deeply in law and technology is to perceive the footfalls of wrestling giants.

Many of the people who study, research, create, and practice law assume that law is poorly situated to address emerging technology. Technology is simply too important, complex, and fast-paced to be subject to deliberate regulation. Others agree that society should fashion rules to shape the direction of technology in the service of human flourishing, but are unsure where to begin.

The social fact of technology has indeed proven remarkably resistant to legal analysis and intervention. The word I like to use is "disorienting." Technology tends to daunt and confuse its observers, with specific consequences for law and legal institutions. Technology hides human will and makes a shell game of responsibility; technology poses as inevitable when it is nearly always contingent; technology invites regulatory paralysis, while placing values and rights into a posture of constant defense. Individually and together, technology's capacity for disorientation poses a special challenge to law and governance to which a successful law and technology analysis must attend.

You can see technological disorientation in Nevada's pioneering driverless car law, which the legislature had to repeal and replace within a year of enacting due to an over-inclusive definition of artificial intelligence (AI). You can see it in a nuclear energy sector that spent three decades without

a plan for disposing of nuclear waste. Technology's disorienting capacity helps explain why many years into the information revolution, the United States lacks any comprehensive privacy law despite overwhelming evidence of harm. It sheds light on the tendency of courts to blame mishaps, accidents, and biases on the people who use tools, instead of those who make them. It presents opportunities for the profit-driven to circumvent law under the banner of disruption.

We legal scholars are not immune to these forces. Our arguments can stale as the technology under examination fails to take the direction we envision. Some fall prey to technological determinism, which imagines a fixed course for technology and reduces complex societal phenomena to the inevitable result of technologic change. We can play into, or even inflate, the challenges around regulating technology, as though other social facts are not just as inscrutable and dynamic.

Notably, many law and technology scholars—that is, the people thinking about the impact of technology on law and legal institutions, or what the rules for technology are or should be—tend to understand their role as restoring the status quo ex ante in light of technological disruption. The bulk of law and technology scholarship to date, while nominally eclectic, shares a common understanding: the role of the legal scholar is to accept extant or anticipated technology and puzzle out how law and legal institutions might adapt to it.

My concern is not necessarily that jurists possess a poor mental model of the inner workings of technology itself. Some readers may be familiar with professor and judge Frank Easterbrook's infamous 1996 address at the inaugural cyberlaw conference at University of Chicago.[7] Facing a gathering of self-identified internet scholars, Judge Easterbrook confidently asserted that there is no more need for a law of cyberspace than for a law of the horse. Regardless, continued the judge and scholar, lawyers are not engineers. Nothing in their training positions the lawyer or law professor to understand technology well enough to comment on it wisely.

While it is true that law professors interested in computers never did "win a Nobel Prize . . . for advances in computer science,"[8] law and technology scholars have proven relatively adept at understanding and explaining the technology under examination. After all, gaining a factual understanding of a new context well enough to argue about it is one of the core skills of lawyering. More and more scholars possess dual training in law and technology, and those that do not, often, partner with colleagues in technical fields. My

concern is a horse of a different color: even tech-savvy lawyers—and many policy-savvy technologists—consistently struggle with technology as a social and cultural phenomenon. Often what we lack is less technical acumen than context.

The problem with legal scholarship about technology is not that jurists or law professors fail to understand how technology works. The problem is that law and technology *as a field* often lacks the rigor, coherence, and consistency that analysis of technology demands. The field has yet to organize itself like other successful areas of legal study—at least not formally. As a consequence, every work at the intersection of law and technology feels sui generis. The field of law and technology to date is poorly situated to address a subject matter as complex, dynamic, and frankly *disorienting* as technology.

The primary goal of the book is to offer a defensible and consistent methodology for the legal analysis of technology. The book holds many insights about both technology and law, garnered from decades of research and practice. But its central contribution is a detailed, step-by-step approach to an important but mercurial subject matter. Whether you are a professor or a student, a lawyer, policymaker, or judge, or simply an intellectually curious reader, this book provides a consistent methodology for successfully analyzing technology from the perspective of law.

An important, secondary goal of the book is to make the case for law and technology as a field. There are many ways law engages in technology—from innovation policy to technology in legal practice. This book is about examining how law anticipates and channels artifacts and systems, that is, what the rules should be *for* and *in light of* technology. No less than health law, or law and economics, law and technology deserves a field of its own. A common methodology, grounded in what most law and technology scholars already do, has the power to confer a sense of coherence and identity upon this burgeoning but disparate field.

There is remarkably little water under this bridge. A few years ago, I was reading a popular listserv for law professors interested in technology, maintained by Mark Lemley at Stanford University. A newer academic posed a question to this group of hundreds: Can anyone recommend a book about how regulators should approach emerging technology? Given the audience, the request should have occasioned an explosion of recommendations (including works by the professors themselves). Instead, it was met with silence. No one recommended anything until someone brought up *Channeling Technology Through Law*,[9] a book on the establishment of the now defunct

Office of Technology Assessment (OTA) by Laurence Tribe. It was published in 1973.

That a request for a book about law and technology would turn up work from fifty years prior, documenting the establishment of a federal agency that no longer exists, astonished me. And led directly to this book. In my research, I found a number of book-length treatments of the interplay between technology and society and several edited volumes dedicated to law and technology themes. I found perhaps a dozen law review articles offering ways to "unify," "structure," "distinguish," or "synthesize" law and technology as a field. But there was no sustained account in the literature of the twenty-first century—an age of innovation and technology—offering students, academics, or policymakers a methodical approach.

I decided to write that account. This book on what law and technology is, and how to go about it, proceeds as follows. The first chapter argues that, for a variety of reasons, technology tends to resist careful and accurate reasoning. Technological disorientation is particularly noteworthy in the context of law, the societal force best positioned to channel technology in the public interest. There is no shortage of discovery and critique around technology. Many disciplines, from philosophy to science and technology studies (STS), examine its social origins and impacts. The law is uniquely situated to do something about it.

The book defines technology in a particular way—as physical or digital artifacts and systems intended to alter human affordances—and describes why technology, so defined, has proven difficult to analyze or restrain. Invoking contemporary and historical examples, and drawing from a variety of other disciplines, Chapter One argues that technology as a concept possesses certain characteristics that tend to lead its observers astray. Consequently, legal analyses of technology are often incomplete, and policymakers either misstep in their efforts to regulate technology or refrain from intervention altogether.

Consider the trope that technology moves too fast for law. In many ways, technology policy of the previous few decades takes place in the shadow of David Collingridge. Collingridge opens *The Social Control of Technology* with the premise that the social and societal ramifications of emerging technology are very difficult to anticipate.[10] Collingridge reasons on this basis that policymakers confronting new technology face a Catch-22. They either intervene too early, before developing an adequate understanding of the technology's direction and ramifications, in which case they do more

harm than good; or, they elect to wait and see, only to find their efforts at channeling the technology stymied by path dependence, public reliance, and the entrenchment of special interests.

For example, a municipality cannot entirely predict how ride-sharing apps (digital services that connect consumers to people willing to drive them around for money) will affect urban transit; so, it humbly waits to regulate them. It turns out that ride-sharing apps can increase traffic, facilitate sexual assault and violent car theft, contribute to mobility inequality, and lure drivers into a false sense of economic security. But by the time the evidence is in, everyone expects to be able to summon a car with their phone, and the leading ride-sharing company spends two million dollars a year on lobbyists (and ten times that on advertising). So, municipalities wind up fashioning rules at the begrudging margins, rules that embrace ride-sharing apps while attempting to mitigate their externalities to acceptable levels.

Through a sort of libertarian magic, the so-called Collingridge dilemma has morphed into the "pacing problem"—a widespread intuition that law cannot keep pace with technology, so it shouldn't bother to try. Law is an old tortoise, technology a restless hare. Accelerating the law is either impossible—legal institutions being famously sclerotic—or ill-advised. The safest course for policymakers is to stand by idly as emerging technology "disrupts" society, and then address the displacement of rights or the advent of significant harms ad hoc.

The logic that technology moves too fast for law is widely accepted. But it is not sound. As an initial matter, technology is far from the only social fact to occasionally outpace the law. In the 1946 Pulitzer-prize winning novel *All the King's Men*, Robert Penn Warren's memorable character Willie Stark likens the law to a blanket that is too small for the bed or else a pair of pants "you bought last year for a growing boy." Stark's diagnosis of the law generally reads like a paraphrase of the pacing problem: "The law is always too short and too tight for growing humankind. The best you can do is do something . . . and by the time that law gets on the books you would have done something different."[11]

Take early twentieth-century attitudes toward alcohol. In 1919, the temperance movement gained such momentum that Americans *amended the Constitution*—the Eighteenth Amendment banning alcohol garnered a supermajority in the House and Senate and was ratified that year by forty-six states. The ban on alcohol rapidly lost support until the Constitution was amended again to reverse prohibition in 1933, but not before widespread

civil resistance. The mid-twentieth century also witnessed a sea change in attitudes toward, and laws around, women and work. Court victories, and laws such as the Fair Labor Standards Act (1938), paved the way for millions of women to enter the labor force, only to be undermined and supplanted a few years later by a perceived need to accommodate servicemen returning from World War II.

Meanwhile, law often keeps up with technology just fine. The United States signed the Outer Space Treaty in 1967, a mere eight years after the first photograph of Earth was taken from orbit. The invention of the Scribner shunt, which made kidney dialysis practicable in the 1960s, led to sweeping changes in health law and policy within a decade.[12] The law is not responsible for the dearth of driverless cars on today's roads or the lack of reliable drone delivery. The National Highway Safety Administration has been interested in the potential of autonomous vehicles since the 1990s. The Federal Aviation Administration created an entire licensure regime around unmanned aerial vehicles years ago at the behest of Congress. The reason we don't have driverless cars or drone delivery as of this writing is because robotics is hard.

By challenging common misconceptions around technology—that technology is apolitical, for example, or moves too fast to be regulated—Chapter One debunks the cloying intuition that law should treat technology any differently than other potential subjects of regulation. If technology differs from other social facts, it is primarily in the *perception* that technology is exceptional. Nevertheless, the incapacity jurists tend to display around new technology indicates the need for a more methodical approach to the field.

Chapter Two addresses the "law" in law and technology, describing what is unique about legal analysis of digital and physical artifacts and systems. A number of disciplines, from the philosophy of technology to STS, explore the nature of technology and its intersection with society. STS, in particular, has examined this intersection in detail using a wide analytic, empirical, and critical toolkit over several decades. Nevertheless, law possesses at least two important distinctions from STS and other fields interested in technology and society: (1) a long-standing comfort with normativity, and (2) a pragmatic understanding of the levers of power.

All but the most committed positivists understand law as unmistakably normative. To write about the law is to suggest or interpret consequential rules governing real people; it is to take positions on how the state ought to resolve conflicts, sometimes by force, involving money, property, freedom, and life itself. Law enjoys, as the saying goes, a monopoly over the legitimate

use of violence. By extension, the people who study and write about law can scarcely avoid discussions of justice. Outside of moral philosophy, perhaps no other academic discipline is quite as focused on what individuals and societies "should" do.

Legal academia is also interested in the specific levers of power—evidencing, in Julie Cohen's words, a "relentless pragmatism" dating back to Oliver Wendell Holmes, Jr. The bulk of books and law review articles on law and technology not only articulate a concern but lay out in detail how best to address it—take *The Future of the Internet and How to Stop It.*[13] We law professors are eager to tell you what you should do about the problem we've identified, and exactly how to do it. This stands in sharp contrast with other academic disciplines that aim to describe our complicated world and the social structures that constitute and attend it, while eschewing normative judgments as unacademic.

The book next develops and defends a methodical approach to law and technology. "[T]o be possessed of a vigorous mind is not enough," writes René Descartes in *Discourse on the Method*, "the prime requisite is rightly to apply it."[14] What was true in 1637 is true today. Approaching problems carefully and consistently are hallmarks of rigorous thought. However fast-paced and dynamic the field appears, I believe that academics and jurists thinking about law and technology will go farther walking slowly down the straight road, than "while they run, forsake it" (id. at 2). I detail my methodology in Chapter Three. At once novel and familiar, the methodology acts as an antidote to the ways technology tends to daunt and mislead the legal observer.

In addition to its promise in addressing the disorienting capacities of technology, I see methodology as key to unifying law and technology as a field. Law as a discipline is hardly monolithic. There are many, splintering subfields, rising and falling with the times. The most successful fields of legal study—in the sense of stable and influential—tend to be organized around either subject matter or method. Examples of the former include health, maritime, and environmental law. Examples of the latter include law and economics, law and literature, and empirical legal studies. Some fields—for example, critical race theory or feminist legal studies—are organized around multiple axes.

Fields can and do organize around the legal dimensions of a common subject. There may be no need for law of the horse; but surely there is need for animal law. Yet, no topic can hold a field together on its own. There are other

essential ingredients, like common knowledge, shared commitments, and communities of learning and practice.

Animal law is not simply the study of the intersection of animals and law. The field traces its origins back to specific court cases and germinal scholarly research from the 1970s. There may be debates among animal law scholars as to whether the best path to animal well-being is through animal rights or welfare. But the field shares a common commitment to questioning and reforming, in Pamela Frasch and Joyce Tischler's words, "a legal system built on the exploitation of beings based on their species."[15] Animal law also benefits from a critical mass of self-described animal law scholars, as well as an annual animal law conference dating back to the 1990s. The same is true, as Chapter Three argues, of health, environmental, privacy, family, maritime, and other areas of law that have stood the test of time.

Interest in a common subject matter is a strong glue. Yet, nothing seems to adhere quite like methodology. Few branches of legal academia have enjoyed an influence on par with law and economics, for example, a field with many formal adherents within and outside the academy. While economic analysis of law may not be, as proponents William Landes and Richard Posner claim, "the most influential development in legal thought since the demise of legal realism in the early 1940s,"[16] there is little question of the movement's considerable impact on scholarship and pedagogy, not to mention judicial and policy decision-making. The influence of law and economics is deeply felt even when it goes unnamed—as when myriad papers on tort law apply cost-benefit or incentive-based analyses without even invoking the field.

Is economics really the soundest basis for legal analysis? Are lawyers well positioned to model economic incentives or parse legal questions in accordance with efficiency? It seems to me that the central advantage of law and economics stems less from its obvious wisdom or even resonance with capitalism than from its adherence to an articulable method. Law as a discipline pays scant attention to methodology.[17] Law review articles do not have methods sections like most journals in humanities and social science, and few legal academics receive formal methods training in law. Simply having a defined goal of efficiency or welfare maximization, let alone a method by which to reach it, confers an enormous advantage.

A handful of legal scholars identify "technology" as their subject matter. Just as many identify themselves as students of the internet, artificial intelligenceAI, robotics, privacy, information, platforms, or innovation.

There are works almost everyone in the field has read—such as Lawrence Lessig's *Code*.[18] Shared commitments are few, however, amounting largely to a general interest in mitigating harms and promoting human flourishing. Only in recent years have there been workshops and conferences specifically organized for law and technology, and many of these emphasize computer science or the application of technology to the practice of law.

Law and technology today is largely organized around a topic. Yet the field of law and technology also possesses certain tactic methods. The majority of law and technology scholarship follows what we might call a *disruption approach*. New technologies often upset assumptions animating law and legal institutions by substituting one way of doing for another. A notable proportion of law and technology scholarship seeks to diagnose the assumptions upended by technology and propose substitutes—legal, technical, or otherwise—that restore the status quo.

The disruption approach in many ways represents an unintended legacy of Lawrence Lessig's *Code*. The ascendance of the commercial internet in the 1990s, which appeared to stand apart from existing social structures, led early theorists to predict an end of the sovereign state. Lessig—who, like Tribe, was a constitutional law scholar who turned his attention for a time to technology—famously rejected this premise. He predicted instead that our collective mediation by technology would shepherd in an era of exquisite control as governments and firms employ their new levers of power.

Lessig developed two crucial ideas that continue to guide contemporary law and technology analysis. First, Lessig postulated that law comprises just one of the four "modalities" of regulation available to powerful institutions—markets, norms, and architecture also secure means to exert control over a population. Even if a virtual or geographically dispersed community cannot be reached by statutes or court orders, it can be governed by the software, hardware, and networks that constitute their underlying architecture. Second, Lessig understood the interaction between law and cyberspace as a function of "latent ambiguities," that is, legal puzzles revealed only when a change in technology alters human habits and capabilities. Thus, for example, Lessig asked if a government computer virus programmed only to reveal unlawful material could constitute a search for purpose of the Fourth Amendment.

Although less remarked than Lessig's mantra that "code is law," the notion that new technologies reveal latent legal ambiguities informed a generation

of legal scholars, myself included. Countless papers in law and technology proceed with the understanding that the role of the law is to identify the ways new technology disrupts prior practice and legal commitments and proposes legal and technical means to reintroduce the values that were lost in the process.

The disruption approach has yielded important insights across a range of contexts. But the approach remains informal, uneven, and piecemeal. The approach makes choices it does not acknowledge, let alone defend, including: the choice of a particular, sometimes arbitrary, instantiation of a technology to analyze, or a focus on an equally specific set of legal commitments that this technology is said to disrupt. The approach also fails to distinguish between the task of governing technology and the effect of technology upon governance. As a consequence, each individual contribution feels sui generis. Few linkages can be made between law and technology projects, even those touching on the same technologies. Larger themes, patterns, and opportunities remain obscure.

Consider, as an example, the accelerating debate over the introduction of machines into the justice system. A series of law review articles and books over the past decade explores the consequences of automating various facets of criminal, civil, and administrative justice. These consequences include the erosion of individual due process guarantees, the reification of gender, class, and racial bias, and the undermining of structural safeguards such as the separation of powers. On the standard account, the "black box" of algorithmic justice simultaneously propagates error and bias while presenting an appearance of objectivity.

This line of study surfaces many of the perils of substituting machines for people and has generated a range of overlapping solutions that, if implemented, would go far in restoring the state of law before the rise of the machines. In some instances, the literature dramatizes flaws in the system that should be remedied quite apart from advances in technology, such as the strange primacy of trade secret law over criminal process. It is good, rigorous, and creative scholarship.

Yet, the entire discourse around machine justice involves a retelling of the same story with different characters. "Many important decisions," the story goes, "historically made by people are now made by computers." This substitution of machines for people breaks certain assumptions held by the law. Though the narrative repeats, each scholar approaches the problem anew by selecting a particular instantiation of the technology (e.g., machine learning)

in a specific context (e.g., administrative hearings). Little more than a loose family resemblance in the artifacts or settings at issue holds the conversation together, let alone connects them to a broader law and technology discourse to draw from and improve. Lost in the mix, meanwhile, is an opportunity to explore key tensions that lie at the heart of machine justice having to do with the affordances of AI relative to people.

Note also how the disruption approach is simultaneously progressive and conservative. The approach feels progressive, in that scholars seem to view technological advancements as inevitable. At the same time, the substitution approach can be understood as conservative, in that it envisions the role of law—and by extension the legal scholar—as restoring the status quo ex ante. The goal is to reproduce safeguards, expectations, and promises in existence before technological change.

A small, if growing, minority of law and technology scholars follow a different path: *technology (tech) assessment.* Tech assessment looks to an earlier stage of development, hoping to understand and anticipate the impacts of emerging technology in service of wiser policymaking. Rather than restore the status quo ex ante with changes to law or code, tech assessment looks to a variety of levers—from research funding to procurement to regulation—for "channeling" technology in the public interest. Tech assessment was the raison d'être of the OTA and the primary subject of Tribe's book. It is also the road not taken in law and technology. Relatively little work in the field, especially in the United States, identifies with the approach of tech assessment as of this writing.[19]

In addition to surfacing assumptions and avoiding pitfalls, a successful methodology for law and technology should be capable of addressing either objective. Chapters 3 and 4 should hold equal interest to those seeking to restore the status quo in light of technological disruption as they do for those hoping to channel new technology in the public interest. Indeed, my hope is that the stages of the method will feel very familiar. My goal in this book is not to foist an entirely new direction on the field than to formalize and strengthen what many already do.

The book then lays out the methodology itself. The four steps of the methodology—definition, envisioning, analysis, and intervention—should feel intuitive to anyone steeped in the literature. But beneath these familiar steps nest a series of prompts and tools designed to aid and formalize our inquiry. A methodical approach to law and technology invites the scholar to make and defend a series of choices, helping to avoid common pitfalls and lend strength and consistency to this rich and important field.

1) *Defining the technology.* The starting place for most law and technology scholarship is fixing the technology under examination. Developing an accurate mental model of a technology is surprisingly difficult, and yet critical to every other step of analysis. Often technology is defined too narrowly or broadly for meaningful engagement, or else commentators conflate a particular, contingent instantiation for the technology itself. Definitions can be idiosyncratic and contested; regardless, they must be concretely stated up front to define the precise scope of inquiry.

A methodical approach to defining technology involves at least three interrelated tasks. The first is determining the *unit of analysis*. Is the scholar writing about a specific technology (e.g., chatbots) or a category (e.g., AI)? The second is identifying what about the technology is essential or *noncontingent*. Google Glass, the heads-up display in a modern fighter jet, and the ghosts in Disney's Haunted Mansion ride are all augmented reality (AR); what do they have in common? The third is distinguishing the artifact or system from previous and constituent technologies. How is this technology new or different?

Presumably law and technology scholarship could focus on the interaction between *any* technology and the legal system. The third task asks the scholar to reflect critically on why they have selected the particular technology for exploration. In some instances, the impetus for examining a given technology will arrive exogenously, as when a member of Congress tasks a staffer with examining a new technology in response to pressure from constituents. But in most, what technology to examine is a choice to be defended.

2) *Envisioning.* Armed with a defensible mental model, this stage explores the concrete ways the technology alters human experience. What avenues of behavior or thought does the technology open, change, or foreclose? Beneath this deceptively simple question are a set of subprompts designed to anticipate and understand technology's individual and societal impacts:

   a. What are the goals and assumptions of the technology's developers? Against what backdrop of culture or perspective does the development occur?
   b. Who are the stakeholders other than technology developers or adopters? How are their experiences and interests affected?

c. Are the risks and advantages of this technology distributed evenly across society? What values or resources does the technology require people or society to sacrifice?
d. Is the change incremental, such that analogy to previous techniques would be appropriate, or does it represent a sea change?
e. What is the timeline for change? Is the change imminent or far off? Is change speculative or reasonably certain?

To lend structure to an admittedly complex and multifaceted inquiry, this stage draws heavily from James Gibson's theory of *affordances*. Increasingly popular in law and technology discourse, affordance theory understands technological change as a function of altering an organism's perception of the environment by changing the environment's capacity to afford opportunity or harm. Thus, for example, a tree affords hiding to a squirrel but not a bear, and a cliff affords danger to people but not to birds. A perceptual psychologist, Gibson developed affordance theory to account for the way organisms perceive an objective environment subjectively. Scholars in other fields—from design theorist Don Norman to sociologist Jenny Davis—have adapted and extended Gibson's insights to describe, respectively, the psychology and politics of everyday things.[20]

Drawing from affordance theory and other methods, such as *value sensitive design*,[21] the second step examines the impacts of emerging technology at the individual, community, and societal or systemic level. The purpose of the exercise is not to predict perfectly how the introduction of technology will play out in society—that is a recipe for technological determinism. But nor does it concede that technology's impacts are entirely unknowable. The goal of this stage is to understand the various ways technology plausibly reshapes human experiences or environments by altering affordances. This is an exercise law and technology already does of necessity, for how else would we have anything meaningful to say, yet in ways that are often tacit and inconsistent. The second stage surfaces those assumptions and lends consistency and rigor to the inquiry.

3) *Analysis*. Assuming a well-defined technical scope—and, more ambitiously, a concrete sense of the ways a new technology stands to alter human affordances—the third stage explores what these changes mean for law and legal institutions. Legal analysis is old hat for law professors. But old hats sometimes need dusting off. The analysis stage

draws from what law and technology scholars already do to lend clarity and rigor to a well-worn but still evolving field. Stages one and two ask, respectively, what distinguishes a new technology from what came before and how that technology changes human affordances. This stage asks the law and technology scholar to announce their path of analysis and state their normative assumptions.

Readers of a certain age may remember the Choose Your Own Adventure books. These books, which send the reader along different paths depending what action they take in the moment, provide a good analogy. The law and technology path most traveled by, at least in the United States, is *technological disruption*, that is, whether certain assumptions of law and policy no longer apply in light of technological change. But there is a second adventure, *tech assessment*, which involves crafting an optimal regime in order to realize the benefits and minimize the harms of a new technology. These approaches speak to different actors, may cite different literatures, and have different motivations. Few works of law and technology say which they are doing.

This stage, like that of definition, encourages transparent engagement with respect to *scope*. Law and technology scholars could look at the impact of a given technology on the law overall. This is rare. An examination of, for instance, AI might focus on one or more particular areas of law such as privacy, copyright, or tort. At most, an AI and law paper will identify cross-doctrinal questions involving personhood or intent, or reexamine the role or nature of agencies, courts, or other institutions in light of AI. The selection of what area of law to analyze is important and interesting; it helps to shed light on the question of what the technology changes for people and society. But most law and technology scholarship launches into legal analysis without attending to scope.

Finally, the analysis stage expects the scholar to articulate a *normative basis* for analysis and, later, prescription. Most law and technology scholars—like legal scholars generally—want their reader to see something as a problem and learn how to fix it. Chapter Two argues that normativity is, along with pragmatism, a discipline-distinguishing feature of legal scholarship. And yet, it is vanishingly rare for a legal scholar to articulate an express normative basis for critique or prescription. Often, the normative basis is the status quo—an existing right or responsibility needing to be restored in light of disruption. Other times, the basis is welfare maximization or antiracism.

This step requires the author's normative basis for worrying about a problem and evaluating a solution to be stated expressly.

4) *Intervention.* The final step focuses pragmatically on solutions and problem solving. Using existing frameworks as points of departure, this stage discusses the various mechanisms by which law and policy can promote the scholar's normative goals in the face of technological change. Levers include everything from new rules or precedents to thoughtful government procurement. Special attention is given to rhetorical choices, which tend to be undertheorized in contemporary law and technology discourse. This section draws from research at the University of Washington's Tech Policy Lab that looks at common pitfalls of tech policy and research, with particular emphasis on the ways technology can negatively impact the vulnerable or marginalized.

The methodical approach offers a way for law professors and lawyers to engage with emerging technology. The emphasis here is analysis, not expression. My hope is that this methodology will yield insights that find their way into books, articles, and essays, but also whitepapers, grant proposals, talks, and even popular writing. I also hope that law and technology will retain its eclectic range of voices. Methodology may yield greater field coherence, but the aim is not homogeneous expression.

Though I anticipate the primary audience for this book to be scholars, students, and practitioners of law and policy, my hope is for the method outlined in Chapter Three to hold value beyond the legal academy. Law has something of a trade deficit with other disciplines. We import insights from economics, literature, sociology, philosophy, neuroscience, and other fields. But these fields seldom refer back to the discoveries and methods of law—how could they, being largely unstated. Disciplines such as STS—wherein more and more scholars are becoming interested not only in diagnosing societal ills, but addressing them—could benefit from the discussions of normative baselining and levers of power. And many disciplines may benefit from greater precision in defining the technology under observation and anticipating its impacts.

The final part of the book applies the preceding insights and methods to past, present, and future examples of technology, and offers thoughts about the direction of the field. Chapter Four applies the methodology to a variety of technologies, selected to span different domains and time periods. By

analyzing a sampling of technologies—AR, AI, and cochlear implants—the chapter demonstrates how to apply a methodical approach to law and technology and why such an approach is useful.

A concluding chapter offers one scholar's reflections on the path of law and technology. The public is waking up to the concerns that technology, while a linchpin of progress, nevertheless threatens human flourishing in ways prosaic and profound. Lawmakers, leaders, and bureaucrats are being asked for solutions. In the United States and abroad, policymakers are rediscovering tech assessment. There are bipartisan efforts to resuscitate the OTA, defunded by Congress in the 1990s during the so-called Gingrich revolution, as a crucial companion to the White House Office of Science and Technology Policy.

This book encourages a rigorous, sober-eyed approach to the study of technology. It eschews Panglossian understandings and resists the urge to accept all technological development as progress. As such, the book may feel at times as though I am skeptical or pessimistic about technology's capacity to lift up humankind. This is not the case. The concluding chapter celebrates technology's capacity to inform, heal, delight, and support. (I don't know what I'd do without the music app Spotify.) More importantly: I would not devote my career to the study of artifacts and systems if I didn't think of them as critical to human flourishing. Technology can and does extend human capabilities well beyond what would seem reasonable for a terrestrial creature. One of the main reasons that the law must get technology right *is* technology's centrality to human experience.

Society needs law and technology both. And law and technology deserves recognition as an important area of study. Formalizing the legal analysis of physical and digital artifacts and systems is the most promising path to meeting society's demands and bring together law and technology as an enduring field. Ultimately, I do not expect that, and indeed would be disappointed if, the methodology I offer were somehow the final say on how law should approach technology. Another advantage of methodology is that every application of a method is an invitation to extend and refine it. My highest hope for this book is that it serves as a point of departure for an ongoing conversation.

On the cover of this book is an ancient dodecahedron, one of several such objects discovered among Roman ruins. Though most observers agree that the artifact holds a purpose beyond decoration—that it represents, in other words, a *technology*—no one is sure what the use may be. Is the

dodecahedron a device for measuring distance? For spooling thread? Is it a child's toy? Answering this question requires more context than history can furnish. The dodecahedron may have been an integral Roman tool. Today it's a curator's paperweight.

The pages that follow discuss many technologies, from a faith-based compass to a system for controlling the weather. But, contemporary or ancient, real or imagined, technology without context is meaningless. People make and use artifacts in particular settings for particular reasons. Those settings and reasons are subject to constraint. If the purpose of technology is expanding the capabilities and affordances of people under the banner of innovation, law's calling is to set the expectations, incentives, and boundaries that channel technology toward human flourishing. This is an admittedly tall order. For law and technology to be up to the task, it must grow from a loose collection of interesting analyses into a careful methodology of its own.

Notes

1. Jameson M. Wetmore, *Amish Technology: Reinforcing Values and Building Community*, 26 IEEE Tech. and Soc'y Mag. (2007).
2. Devil's Playground (Cinemax 2002).
3. Alex Vadukul, *'Luddite' Teens Don't Want Your Likes*, N. Y. Times (Dec. 15, 2022), https://www.nytimes.com/2022/12/15/style/teens-social-media.html (last visited Jan. 13, 2025).
4. Amy Sue Bix, *"Remember the Sabbath": A History of Technological Decisions and Innovation in Orthodox Jewish Communities*, 36 Hist. & Tech. 205 (2020).
5. The term "social fact" is often associated with Émile Durkheim. In *The Rules of Sociological Method*, Durkheim defines social facts as "a category of facts which . . . consist of manners of acting, thinking and feeling external to the individual, which are invested with a coercive power by virtue of which they exercise control over him." Émile Durkheim, The Rules of Sociological Method (Steven Lukes 1982) (1895). My use of the term is closer to that of science and technology studies (STS), which recognizes the ways technology shapes, and is shaped by, society.
6. Bruno Latour, *Technology Is Society Made Durable*, 38 Socio. Rev. 103 (1990).
7. Frank H. Easterbrook, *Cyberspace and the Law of the Horse*, 1996 U. Chi. Legal F. 207 (1996).
8. Which would be hard, as there is no such prize. The reference is to the *Law of the Horse* speech Judge Easterbrook delivered at the University of Chicago School of Law at an early cyberlaw conference, questioning the utility of an area of study devoted to law and the internet. *See id.* at 207.
9. Laurence H. Tribe, Channeling Technology Through Law (Bracton Press 1973).
10. David Collingridge, The Social Control of Technology (Cambridge University Press 1980). The idea that the impacts of technology cannot be anticipated has been ironically bolstered by STS scholars seeking to disprove a second myth, that technology has inevitable characteristics or impacts (so-called technological determinism).
11. Robert Penn Warren, All the King's Men (Harcourt, Brace, & Co. 1946).
12. Sallie Thieme Sanford, *What Scribner Wrought: How the Invention of Modern Dialysis Shaped Health Law and Policy*, 13 Rich. J. L. & Pol'y 337 (2010).
13. Jonathan Zittrain, The Future of the Internet and How to Stop It (Yale University Press 2008).
14. René Descartes, Discourse on the Method of Rightly Conducting One's Reason and of Seeking Truth in the Sciences (1637), 1.

15. Joyce Tischler & Pamela Frasch, *Animal Law: The Next Generation*, 25 Animal L. Rev. 303 (2019).
16. William M. Landes & Richard A. Posner, *The Influence of Economics on Law: A Quantitative Study*, 36 J. L. & Econ. 385 (1993).
17. Years ago, then Harvard Law School Dean Martha Minow developed a "field guide" to legal scholarship to which many in the academy still refer. The field guide lists various categories of scholarly engagement, from doctrinal restatement to critical or comparative projects, and describes their core characteristics. The word "method" arises once, in passing. Martha Minow, *Archetypal Legal Scholarship: A Field Guide*, 63 J. Legal Educ. 65 (2013).
18. Lawrence Lessig, Code and Other Laws of Cyberspace (Basic Books 1999).
19. Versions of the public interest vary. Some work in the critical tradition, which would dismantle techno-social structures entirely as paternalistic, colonial, or racist, may not identify as tech assessment. Yet these accounts share with tech assessment the broader goal of channeling technology from the outset, rather than merely restoring the status quo in light of substitution.
20. Donald A. Norman, The Design of Everyday Things: Revised and Expanded Edition (Basic Books 2013) (1988); Jenny L. Davis, How Artifacts Afford: The Power and Politics of Everyday Things (MIT Press 2020).
21. Batya Friedman & David G. Hendry, Value Sensitive Design: Shaping Technology with Moral Imagination (MIT Press 2019).

Suggested Readings

David Collingridge, The Social Control of Technology (Cambridge University Press 1980).

Jenny L. Davis, How Artifacts Afford: The Power and Politics of Everyday Things (MIT Press 2020).

Lawrence Lessig, *The Law of the Horse: What Cyberlaw Might Teach*, 113 Harv. L. Rev. 501–549 (1999).

Lyria Bennett Moses, *How to Think about Law, Regulation and Technology: Problems with 'Technology' as a Regulatory Target*, 5 L., Innovation & Tech. 1 (2013).

Jameson M. Wetmore, *Amish Technology: Reinforcing Values and Building Community*, 26 IEEE Tech. and Soc'y Mag. (2007).

ONE

TECHNOLOGY AS SOCIAL FACT

Introduction

The historian Leo Marx refers to technology as a "hazardous concept." Marx's claim is not that a particular instantiation of technology is dangerous. He sees danger in the very idea. Marx traces a rhetorical shift at the turn of the twentieth century when technology came to be a kind of shorthand for the desirable inevitability of industrial progress. Today it seems a truism that "technology is changing the way we live," as though technology were a free-standing societal force rather than a collection of social and material choices. "By attributing autonomy and agency to technology," Marx writes in 1997, "we make ourselves vulnerable to the feeling that our collective life in society is uncontrollable."[1]

Society does not treat technology like other social facts. Whereas many have come to recognize religion, race, or gender as highly contingent—beholden to history and culture—technology continues to feel inevitable and apart from the social and societal forces that shape it. Other social facts change; technology *advances.*

The technology du jour artificial intelligence (AI) serves as an excellent case in point. In *Atlas of AI*, Kate Crawford explores the ways AI casts a spell of "enchanted determinism" over proponent and critic alike. Enthusiasts mystify the inner workings of AI even as they offer up its potential to solve any problem. AI can never be understood but it can always help. Yet detractors fall into a similar trap for Crawford, "blam[ing] algorithms for their negative outcomes as though they were independent agents, without contending with the contexts that shape them and in which they operate." "Both the tech utopians and dystopians frame the problem with technology always at the center," she concludes, "inevitably expanding into every part of life [and] decoupled from the forms of power that it magnifies and serves."[2]

This chapter concerns the specific ways technology tends to mislead and confuse people and institutions, including those people and institutions who make, study, and argue about the law. Over the years I have observed (and

Law and Technology. Ryan Calo, Oxford University Press. © Ryan Calo 2025.
DOI: 10.1093/9780197526170.003.0002

committed!) any number of mistaken assumptions and beliefs about technology that stand in the way of adequate legal analysis.

First: technology poses as inevitable even when it is deeply contingent. Whatever technology we happen to observe or experience, from the nuclear power plant to the delivery robot, represents but one of many possible instantiations. Yet many law review articles, court decisions, and regulations proceed as though the artifact or system that happened to reach the market could be configured in no other way. Wherever technology goes, that was where it was headed. A corollary to this phenomenon is the tendency to assume technology is the sole factor behind social change or will only change those narrow aspects of society—e.g., who is driving a car or writing a story—at which the technology was directed.

Second: technology can hide human will and make a shell game of responsibility. Technology tends to render the existence and impact of certain constraints, choices, and "politics" harder to detect. When we do something with or through technology, we may not be aware of the ways the designers of that technology are channeling our behavior. We may not see their biases, assumptions, and goals. And when technology causes harm in the world, it can be very difficult to sort out who is responsible or even who is involved. Whatever human happens to be on hand becomes a scapegoat or "moral crumple zone," assuming a human can even be found to blame.[3]

Third: technology, especially emerging technology, appears difficult or undesirable to regulate. Technology is too complicated for inexpert policymakers to understand, too fast for law to keep up. Technology's impacts on society cannot be anticipated well enough to control; they must be allowed to play out unimpeded. Technology is the golden goose of progress, promising to fix big problems while boosting the economy and keeping us safe from rivalrous nations. Technology "disrupts" prevailing norms and expectations, displacing old ways of thinking. The optimism that attends technology is nothing short of startling. Technology's benefits are assumed. Its failures to address societal ills, from global education inequality to digital contact-tracing during a pandemic, get elided or ignored.

After defining technology in a particular way—as physical or digital artifacts or systems designed to alter human affordances—this chapter explores technology's troubling characteristics, using scholarly and real-world examples to illustrate the consequences.

Drawing from case studies, from driverless cars to the internet, the pages that follow explore a variety of flawed takes, missed opportunities, and

technology policy breakdowns that flow directly from technological disorientation. Diagnosing the impediments through clear thinking about the social fact of technology has independent value in helping scholars, policymakers, and jurists to be more vigilant. But ultimately, this chapter makes the case for a methodical approach to law and technology capable of attending to technology's capacity to confuse and mislead.

What Is Technology?

Stuck at a red light, I watched a crow dive down toward the pavement, rising at the last moment only to repeat the motion. Just as the light changed, the behavior suddenly became clear: the bird was using gravity and momentum to smash a nut against the street to break it open.

Chimpanzees in Nouabalé-Ndoki National Park in the Republic of Congo, have been observed to make and carry ant-foraging "kits" with a dozen specialized tools for opening nests or sucking up insects before they can bite or sting. Army ants build bridges out of their very bodies, sacrificing hundreds so that thousands can cross rifts in leaf cover.

The Book of Mormon makes repeated references to an instrument, the Liahona, an intricate brass compass with several spindles. According to the Church of Latter-day Saints, the Liahona guided the prophet Lehi and his fellow travelers through the wilderness and over the ocean but ceased to function the moment they lost faith.

On the cover of this book is an ancient Roman artifact whose purpose has been lost to time.

Are each of these examples of "technology"? Artifacts fashioned by people or other animals from surrounding materials to extend their capabilities seem like rather obvious examples. But what of the highflying crow, which created neither gravity nor the hard pavement? What of the ant that uses its own body as a bridge? What of the Liahona, or, for that matter, a lucky rabbit's foot?

There are many candidates for what constitutes technology. A recurrent theme in the philosophy of technology is that technology represents the reduction of science to practice. To paraphrase Herbert Simon in *The Sciences of the Artificial*, science concerns itself with what is, technology with what can be.[4] This definition distinguishes technology from scientific theory or the scientific method, which yields insights that require independent

application to have a direct impact on human experience. The condition that it leverage science also tends to distinguish technology from decorative arts and crafts. In contrast, science and technology studies (STS) tends to problematize any distinction between science and technology, understanding both as aspects of the same set of social constructs. Science and technology are both examinable human behaviors.

Many definitions understand technology to involve, if not science, then the pragmatic organization of knowledge. Some theorists (notably, Jacques Ellul) analyze technology at the level of "technique," in the sense of any rationalized effort to enhance a human activity.[5] Ruha Benjamin conceives of race—"one of our most powerful tools"—as a kind of technology of domination.[6]

Others require a degree of materiality, of "thingness," to meet their definition. Thus, for example, Frederick Ferré begins with the deceptively simple premise that technology consists of "practical implementations of intelligence." Yet Ferré goes on to stipulate that technology cannot be "empty-handed," or exist only in the mind of the participant. It must be embodied in a tool or system.[7] Bruno Latour suggests a connection to materiality as well when he refers to technology as "society made durable." Latour is interested in the ways societal assumptions, such as the naturalness of the nuclear family, find stability in artifacts, such as the single-family home with a yard and picket fence.[8]

For purposes of this book, I will understand technology as necessarily embodied in physical or digital artifacts and systems. Technology is not synonymous with science, in the sense of organized production of knowledge, nor with technique, in the sense of deliberate or rational processes. I concede to the philosophers that all of these concepts are closely related. Technique produces technology and technology supports technique—microscopes enable the science from which they are born. But my focus throughout the book is on how the law interacts with *things*, not ways.

The classic dichotomy between technology and nature is as difficult to police as that between technology and technique. My own sense, however, is that technology must involve conscious artifice. A chameleon's camouflage is not a technology, for example, nor are the psychotropic qualities of certain mushrooms. I will talk about technology as something we create in order to do. Just as an arresting sunset is not art, however pregnant with meaning, so a naturally occurring phenomenon is not technology on my account. The idea that technology involves artifice is also reflected in laws governing

human innovation, as when patent law resists protecting phenomena already occurring in nature.

I am not committed to the idea that technology must work as intended, or at all. Estimates suggest that up to a fifth of drug prescriptions in the United States are for indications not approved by the Food and Drug Administration, so called "off label" uses. For example, doctors prescribe hypertension drugs to treat nightmares or performance anxiety. If I want to drive a little nail into my office wall to hang a picture, it would be nice to have a hammer. But I am perfectly happy to use the bottom of my stapler. A road is hard not because it cracks nuts, but because cars have to drive on it and rain must skitter off. Yet that hardness turns out to be of use to the hungry crow.

Broken technology is technology. Failed technology is too. Were humans to discover an abandoned interstellar spaceship we couldn't operate—or, less exotically, an ancient Roman dodecahedron made of bronze for which no one can fathom a use—the word "technology" still seems to fit. These are artifacts created for the purpose of extending capabilities. Some may even be comfortable applying the label where functionality is a matter of faith, so long as the intent to act on the world is present.

Technology is a non-natural social fact of a particular kind. Technology is non-natural, insofar as it consists of the artifacts and systems we fashion out of our environment. I understand technology can be made up of inert or biological material, as well as signals and data. But it is not just the natural world itself. Technology is social in the sense that it is both shaped by social and societal forces, and shapes them in turn—an insight I evidence throughout this book by drawing heavily from the field of STS. Unlike many social facts, such as marriage or religion, instances of technology are reduced to specific material forms.

With this in mind, here is my working definition: *Technology consists of any physical or digital artifact or system designed to alter affordances or to extend capabilities, irrespective of whether the artifact or system manages to do so.*

I have defined technology in these terms, as altering and extending affordances, because I am specifically interested in what makes technology challenging to law. As Lyria Bennett Moses, Margot Kaminski, Meg Leta Jones, and others observe, technology is interesting to law if and when it affects what people are able to do or how they do it. Outside of certain corners of intellectual property, the question is less what technology is, than what it changes.

Law often finds the social fact of technology challenging precisely because human aspiration or intent has been reduced to artifact. When two people collude to fix prices, the Department of Justice seldom struggles to apply the Sherman Act. Yet, legal scholars write entire articles and books on the topic of "algorithmic collusion," that is, the emergent synchronization of prices by independent algorithms.[9] The Federal Trade Commission (FTC) has policed deceptive advertising for a hundred years. But only recently has the agency explored how the very design of a website may constitute a "dark pattern" capable of deceiving or manipulating the consumer without words.

Technology is a social fact like any other, but one with a particular set of properties, each wrapped up in the way technology reduces human intent to discrete, digital or physical objects. The remainder of the book understands technology in terms of the practical and useful artifacts and systems people make and use.

Technology's Hazards

In 2010, a lobbyist for the technology company Google approached the state of Nevada with a proposal: legalize driverless cars and Google will test its fleets there, positioning the state as a leader in the future of transportation. Nevada's breathless lawmakers soon passed legislation permitting the testing of driverless cars within certain parameters and in accordance with special rules. The pioneering law restricted but blessed vehicles controlled by "artificial intelligence," which Nevada defined as a computer taking over the function of a human driver. This definition suited Google just fine, since the company's vision involved fully autonomous fleets of vehicles that converted mobility into a service consumers could summon on demand.

It turns out Nevada's definition did not work for everyone. Luxury vehicle manufacturers, in particular, became very concerned that the law—which required, for example, putting up a large bond for each vehicle in case of accidents—would reach high-end cars already on the market. These cars used AI to park themselves and nudge inattentive drivers back into their lane. The legacy automobile companies had an entirely different vision than did Google for autonomous vehicles, in which cars would continue to take over various driving functions in a series of planful stages. Scrutiny mounted until, a year after passing the first driverless car law in America, Nevada had to repeal the statute and rewrite it.

Nevada fell into one of several powerful traps technology lays for the unwary. The state is not alone. Be they lawmaker, student, or longtime academic, technology as a social fact has a tendency to daunt and confuse its observers. Over the years, I have observed three attributes of technology in particular that interfere with our capacity to understand and respond: (1) non-contingence, (2) hidden will, and (3) ungovernability. The legal analysis of technology must attend to these and other ways technology feels different than other social facts, resulting in real consequences for law and legal institutions.

Non-contingence

The opening pages of this book allude to a critical way technology confuses and misleads observers: technology poses as inevitable when in fact it is nearly always contingent.

There is a widely shared intuition that technology evolves, improving with each iteration. The driverless car is the obvious next step in personal transportation, freeing up time and urban space while reducing fatalities. It is rare for the American or any other government to fundamentally question whether a new technology improves upon the status quo. There are exceptions—for example, President George W. Bush's 2001 ban on federal funding for stem cell research, or more recent municipal moratoria on facial recognition technology—but politicians and bureaucrats tend to see their role in technology policy as supporting innovation in the service of progress. The Department of Transportation has been working with a shifting cadre of companies to support the development of driverless vehicles since, at least, the 1990s. In 2012, Congress ordered the Federal Aviation Administration (FAA) to integrate drones into the American airspace; ten years later, the Government Accountability Office chastised the FAA for failing to do so.

I will return to the perils of unquestioning acceptance of new technology shortly. I want to focus for now on a second aspect of non-contingence: the tendency of legal scholars and jurists to fixate upon a particular instantiation of technology that the market or the media has placed before them. The introduction of a specific new product into the market limits legal analysis by fixing that particular configuration of the technology in the popular, and legal, imagination. The object of study or regulation becomes *this thing*—the driverless car, the delivery robot, the drone, the virtual currency, the

augmented reality headset, the AI chatbot—rather than the bundle of technological affordances that constitute these systems. Google's driverless car presents as a unified, incontrovertible whole, rather than a set of sensors, actuators, and processors that might have also been combined in a different way—for example, to automate buses in a bid to resuscitate public transportation.

The idea that the technology we experience is inevitable, rather than contingent, has tangible consequences for technology governance. Legal commentators do not recognize, in new technology, a reconfigurable bundle of affordances so much as a specific product with immoveable features. The subject of study and regulation becomes what to do about *the* driverless car Google let federal officials and Nevada lawmakers ride in, rather than the novel possibilities for automation in transportation that the sensors and AI powering these cars afford. How else might Nevada move people and resources around the state with robotics? We may never know.

Robots make for an excellent case study. Robots are, in essence, machines that can sense their environment, process what they sense, and then act upon the world. Differences among robots are largely a product of the number and sophistication of their component parts—their sensors, processors, or actuators. Robots range enormously in capability and morphology (shape and style), from the mechanical wind-up robot in my office that can sense the edge of the table and turn itself to avoid falling off, to ATLAS, the bipedal, humanoid robot developed by Boston Dynamics that incorporates the latest in hydraulics and machine learning to perform literal gymnastics.

The task of the law is to grapple with the full range of affordances offered by robotics, not to pass a series of rules for each robot the press happens to cover. Yet, regulators do precisely the latter.

In 2013, I was asked to testify before the Judiciary Committee of the United States Senate on the privacy concerns posed by drones in law enforcement. Immediately prior to the hearing, the Senators were treated to a demonstration: a company showed off a quadcopter of the sort being marketed to the police. The drone spent the remainder of the hearing on a table in plain view of attendees and C-SPAN.

As I explained to the Senators, the privacy harm of drones flows primarily from their ability to follow people inexpensively or peer into private spaces from a public vantage. This capability is not limited to the drones law enforcement uses today, but represents a broader concern related to developments in digital and kinetic technology. Congress should address the

question of cheap mobile surveillance holistically, I argued, agnostic as to the technology. I and others made the same point to state lawmakers in meetings and to the general public in op-eds.

The legislation most states passed—and all but one wise federal bill[10]—did not target the problem of cheap mobile surveillance that flight, automation, and high-definition cameras afford. These laws and bills tackled *drone* surveillance, defined very specifically to include unmanned fixed-wing or rotor aircraft like the one sitting on the Senate chambers table. Most laws made explicit reference to the FAA's rules defining "unmanned aerial systems" in similar terms.

The years since 2013 have seen many different configurations of high-definition recording and mobility—private satellites, a robot that climbs the side of a building, a robot that can leap thirty feet high, a ball-camera that officers throw into the air to take 360° panoramic pictures of crowds—that present-day legislation does not reach despite their functional equivalence to drones. Lawmakers proved unable to imagine, let alone anticipate, anything other than the products specific companies and the media first surfaced.

The same pattern can be seen in robot-based delivery. Around 2015, an Estonian company called Starship Technologies began to pilot a fleet of autonomous wheeled robots that travel the sidewalk to deliver goods. The robots have six wheels and weigh about forty pounds. Like Google, Starship Technologies approached a variety of jurisdictions about legislation that would formally permit their robots while imposing certain restrictions. Many states passed laws blessing precisely the lightweight, wheeled configuration that Starship Technologies placed before them. These innovation-promoting laws ironically locked in one mode of automated delivery over the many other ways robots could move goods around a city.

These are just a few recent examples involving one technology. Lawmakers have enacted or proposed laws specific to a wide range of technologies—from smart meters to license plate readers, from shared scooters to pea shooters—rather than trying to address the underlying concerns of privacy or safety these technologies present by altering what humans are able to do.

The dominant strain of American law and technology scholarship also understands technological change as inevitable. Many law and technology scholars aim their analysis at whatever specific instantiation of technology the market happened to yield, or they read about in the tech section of the New York Times (a reliable citation in any law and technology article). These scholars understand their task as discovering what assumptions of law and

policy no longer obtain in light of the disruption, and fashioning new rules to restore the status quo ex ante.

Once upon a time, people with driver's licenses and individual car insurance drove cars. Now, cars apparently drive themselves. What changes to law and legal institutions may be necessary to encourage safe driving and compensate injured victims? Integrating this instinct—that the task of law and technology is to adapt law to technological disruption—with its alternatives—that law can have an active role in shaping the development and path of technology from the outset—is a major theme of this book.

Thus, the problem of the apparent non-contingency of new technology is twofold. First, society only bothers to address a subsection of issues a new technology presents, as jurists and academics lavish attention on whatever instantiation of the technology the market or the press happen to place before them. Future configurations or uses of the technology may cause the same or greater harm but go unaddressed because the public and academy have moved on. Second, technological change consistently presents society with *opportunities* to alter how we live. These opportunities never surface due to contingent design choices made before any policymaker or the public was able to think through the range of possibilities presented by new technological affordances. We don't think in terms of what could be technologically, but what happens to be.

Closely related to the acceptance of particular instantiations of technology as inevitable is the belief that technology invariably drives social change of a specific kind—what STS calls "technological determinism." As a social fact, technology has the capacity to shape social and societal relations, sometimes profoundly. Yet, the development and adoption of technology is itself shaped by people and institutions in multifaceted ways. We'll see later in the chapter that taking this insight too far can lead to regulatory paralysis: if there is no way to predict what technology will do, how can governments make rules in advance? Failing to acknowledge that technology is only part of any story of change has led many in the field astray.

Law professor Orin Kerr's influential theory of the Fourth Amendment holds that the introduction of new technology can upset the balance between the capacities of law enforcement and criminals, leading judges to reinterpret the Warrant Clause of the Constitution to restore the status quo through a process of "equilibrium adjustment." When technology gives the bad guys an edge, Kerr reasons, courts change their interpretation of "unreasonable search or seizure" to restore balance.[11] This is an interesting argument.

The invention of the motor vehicle may have changed the affordances of bootleggers, who could suddenly hide contraband in the trunk of a fast-moving automobile. Yet, the argument is woefully incomplete. Is not a more plausible candidate for the tectonic shift in our understanding of the Fourth Amendment in the early twentieth century, which included relaxing search and seizure law around vehicles, the sudden necessity of trying to stop millions of Americans from drinking?

Another sort of error arises when legal scholars assume that technology will shape behavior in a single, inevitable way. Early examinations of online speech or digital copyright, for example, acknowledged the technical capacity of the internet to reduce barriers to information sharing by facilitating "cheap speech." But few foresaw how the internet would change the very nature of content, markets, and firms.[12] (Some did. I remember how odd it seemed for a company that mailed you physical DVDs to be called "Netflix," until all content delivery began to stream over the internet.) Importantly, among the most fundamental changes to human life—for example, the gutting of the American shopping mall, or the rise of telework and telemedicine—occurred as the affordances of the internet interacted with a socio-biological phenomenon, such as a global pandemic.

Torts scholars examining the liability implications of driverless cars tend to hold constant all other aspects of car ownership and use but for who or what is doing the driving—AI, instead of people. Notwithstanding the fact that investment comes mostly from technology firms whose business model involves turning everything into an on-demand service, driverless cars on this story are still individually owned and operated; law need only apply enterprise, products, or strict liability to account for the shift in responsibility for operation from the occupant to the engineers and their employer. The solutions on offer commonly fail to anticipate how the introduction of fully driverless cars could effectuate a sea change in personal mobility. Thus, they tend not to explore how the model of transportation as service may affect tort liability overall.

This tendency to acknowledge technological but not social change calls to mind the science fiction of the 1950s, within which characters commute to Mars in futuristic spaceships but are still being waited on by feminine stewardesses in short skirts.

This feeling of *inevitability* and non-contingency is the hazard against which Leo Marx warns, and why I assign work about Amish technology adoption to my students. And this is why law and policy—at least in twenty-first

century United States—takes existing artifacts and systems as its starting point, asking how law and legal institutions should adapt to their specific disruptions. As future chapters explore, the successful methodology for the legal analysis of technology must be capable of both resisting and accommodating this impulse—understanding what assumptions of law and policy a given configuration of technology challenges, yes, but also taking changes in technology as an invitation to inventory and advance human values.

Hidden will

A second way technology daunts and confuses legal observers is by making a shell game of responsibility. The use of technology to accomplish various tasks introduces the assumptions, biases, and intentions—conscious or otherwise—of the people and groups that created the technology. This insight has been expressed in many ways by many people, and yet the basic idea—that technology means *someone else not present is participating*—continues to pose deep challenges for legal analysis.

There is, of course, widespread recognition that blame can flow to the creators of faulty technology. Products liability plays an enormous role in torts, for example, as most of the ways people get hurt involve things. Not only can an individual's use of technology, such as a deadly weapon, make a crime more serious, but sometimes courts will hold manufacturers liable for making a product that is too easy to misuse—as when an ordinary gun can be converted into a semi-automatic assault weapon with a simple attachment.

Some affordances of technology—the ability to act at a distance, for example, or speak with anonymity—can make it harder to identify perpetrators and establish guilt. The availability of near-untraceable virtual currency helped fuel an epidemic of ransomware attacks, wherein distant hackers infiltrate a network and hold a business hostage by encrypting its data. Other capabilities allow many people to coordinate harmful behavior, as when many actors engage in a denial-of-service attack by deluging an internet server with requests to connect. Conversely, surveillance or forensic technology can help solve crimes that would have baffled prior generations of investigators. None of this is particularly vexing to law.

A more difficult legal question arises when complex machines display "emergent" behavior, that is, take actions that are not reasonably predictable

even to the system's designers.[13] The very value of such systems often lies in their unexpected, useful adaptation: an AI trained to play chess invents a new opening that changes how grandmasters play the game. A problem arises for law when adaptive behavior by machines engages in legitimately unexpected behavior that would constitute a crime or a tort if a person did it. Criminal, tort, and many other areas of law generally will not find fault where no human being could reasonably have foreseen the result. Unless jurists are careful, technology in such circumstances can confuse liability by raising the prospect of victims without perpetrators.

Imagine, for example, an "intelligent" hybrid vehicle that is designed not only to drive itself but to experiment with its internal state to optimize energy efficiency. The engineers set certain safety parameters, such as the requirement that the vehicle obey traffic laws and respond to manual overrides of any system. Otherwise, the car is free to adapt. Imagine this vehicle discovers that it always performs better, energy-wise, if it starts the day with a full battery. One evening the owners of the car park it in their garage and forget to plug it in. No problem, "thinks" the car, and runs the gas engine at night to charge its battery—poisoning the owners sleeping inside the house with carbon monoxide. (Computers famously do what you say, not what you want.)

The car engineers would feel horrible; society would lay the blame at their feet. But in court, they could credibly argue against liability due to the absence of proximate causation. In tort, the element of proximate causation famously requires the plaintiff to show that the harm alleged was foreseeable to a reasonable person or professional. Early lawsuits against asbestos manufactures foundered because no one knew or had reason to know at the time of sale that the material caused lung disease. Showing proximate causation is required, even in cases of so-called "strict" liability where the court otherwise assumes fault by the defendant. The engineers could plausibly argue that asphyxiation as a category of harm, let alone this specific behavior, was not something they could reasonably have foreseen before the first time it happened.

As machines become more adaptive, interacting in complex ways with the environment and with one another, judges and juries will grapple with how to allocate responsibility for machine behavior in the absence of intent or proximate causation by a human being. Pinning blame for anything the machine does on its creator is not consonant with legal principles as they stand today, and undermines what makes these systems special—their ability to solve problems without human supervision and in ways people cannot

fathom. But the absence of liability provides no comfort to the victims of emergent behavior, who experience a machine that has decided to hurt them.

Nevertheless, I am not overly worried over such puzzles. American law is itself adaptable; new doctrines can evolve from statutory or common law to solve questions, such as liability for emergent behavior. My focus here is on the broader and long-standing incapacity of jurists to see clearly in a different context involving technology. I am worried about the many situations where design choices smuggle in the designer's worldview, quietly channeling user behavior to particular ends. It is through this set of phenomena that analysis breaks down and technology confuses responsibility.

"In controversies about technology and society," writes Langdon Winner in his 1980 article *Do artifacts have politics?*, "there is no idea more provocative than the notion that technical things have political qualities." Using a series of examples, Winner demonstrates how technical decisions can embed the "politics" of engineers and designers into the artifacts and physical structures of everyday life.[14] The decision of urban architect Robert Moses to connect New York City to the suburbs via bridges too low for public buses reflects, on Winner's account, Moses's alleged politics of racialized class segregation.[15] The invention of the tomato harvester, which only works on tomatoes bred to be firm, elevated the value of efficiency over taste and nutrition. The invention of the submarine undermined the laws of war, for example, that once obligated an enemy to rescue sailors from a felled ship.

Even subtle architectural choices can have robust effects on behavior. I remember watching footage of the January 6, 2021, riots at the United States Capitol following the defeat of President Donald Trump. The rioters scaled fences, assaulted officers, and broke windows to gain access to the building. Once inside, however, interior cameras show the crowds moving from room to room dutifully staying within the velvet ropes set up for tourists.

It took well over a decade, but the cyberlaw community—notably Joel Reidenberg and Lawrence Lessig—rediscovered this argument in the context of the internet.[16] A number of scholars argued that the design of digital systems constrains and channels behavior at least as much as legal rules, an idea canonized in the insight that "code is law." Lessig uses the very same example as Winner—Moses's overpass to Long Island—to illustrate how architecture operates as a "modality" of regulation, alongside law, norms, and market forces. The idea that code regulates the internet has become a bedrock principle of law and technology with an increasingly diverse set of scholars exploring the many ways architectural and design decisions

constrain or channel online behavior, often toward the goals of governments, corporations, or other powerful institutions.

Despite the long-standing scholarly attention to the basic idea that technology smuggles in human will via design, policymakers, judges, and even a few academics, too, continue to characterize technology as fundamentally neutral or open-ended.[17] Perhaps certain technologies, such as flamethrowers or cigarettes, are imbricated with danger, they concede. Yet, for most harms involving technology, many legal commentators still follow the intellectual equivalent of "guns don't kill people; people kill people." Contemporary technologies are human tools: they reason, and humans decide whether and how to use these tools.

Some of the ways engineering decisions hide human will are, or become, obvious. Consider again the context of vehicles. In 2015, the Environmental Protection Agency fined the German car manufacturer Volkswagen for programming its diesel vehicles to evade emissions testing. The cars were designed to sense when they were being tested and initiate a protocol that emitted about 40 times less nitrous oxide than real-world driving conditions. Until a group of independent researchers discovered the deception, the people testing Volkswagen emissions did not appreciate that someone else was present—exerting intentional control over the situation through carefully concealed code.

Other ways are still harder to see. American transportation is undergoing a transition involving automation; exactly how it will play out remains anyone's guess. But as vehicles rely more on software and less on people, courts and regulators have struggled with who bears the blame for accidents. The luxury electric vehicle manufacturer Tesla designed into its vehicles a self-driving feature called "Autopilot." The system has seen deadly failures—in 2016, for example, the vehicle mistook a white trailer for the bright sky and ran directly into it. Yet, despite the imperfections in engineering—not to mention the choice of name—the company placed responsibility on the victim. "Autopilot is getting better all the time," Tesla said in a statement, "but it is not perfect and still requires the driver to remain alert."

Similarly, when an autonomous vehicle designed by the ride-sharing company Uber struck and killed a pedestrian crossing the street outside the crosswalk, the local prosecutor brought charges not against Uber, but against the woman Uber had hired to monitor the vehicle. This despite a report by the National Transportation Safety Board concluding that Uber possessed an "ineffective safety culture," and had made avoidable mistakes

in the vehicle's architecture. What neither the federal nor local government questioned, however, is how realistic it is to expect even a paid employee to pay complete attention in a car designed to drive hours upon hours without driver intervention.

There is a pronounced tendency to blame people who are proximate in place and time to technology. Consumer protection law scholar David Vladeck studied litigation around accidents involving autopiloting systems.[18] He found that courts in such cases would look for a responsible person, rather than grapple with the role of the machine. In one airplane crash case, for example, the record established that there had been an issue with the airplane's automated navigation system. But there was also a suggestion that airline employees had loaded the plane improperly, causing it to be off balance. Though airplanes are presumably misloaded from time to time without serious consequences, the court focused on the conduct of the human beings who maintained the airplane, to the exclusion of the engineers who built it. This had the consequence of shifting liability away from the distant manufacturer toward the immediately present airline and airport staff.

For anthropologist Madeleine Elish, humans run the risk of becoming superfluous components of automated systems, inserted to act as a kind of "moral crumple zone."[19] Just as a car may be longer than necessary to absorb the impact of a collision and protect the occupants, Elish argues, so might technical systems include humans in the loop to absorb the blame and liability for accidents. This concerning strategy would not be plausible but for a widespread technological incapacity—our failure to guess correctly in the shell game of technological responsibility.

I have made a case study of vehicles for consistency. But the problem of hidden will extends well beyond planes and cars. Some of the most vivid examples arise within digital systems like the internet or virtual reality. For centuries, it felt accurate to speak about technology as something people work *with* in order to accomplish goals. Increasingly, technology is something *through* which we live, love, work, and create. Technology is more of an environment than a tool. That we are mediated—through browsers, phones, headsets, and other systems—dramatically increases the prospect that our perception and behavior will be overtly and subtly channeled by the engineers of experience. Today's digital, algorithmically curated environments routinely embed invisible values in ways that continue to escape notice and defy legal analysis.

Mediated environments embed the assumptions of their designers. A generation of urban planners grew up playing SimCity—a thirty-year-old videogame wherein players design and maintain a virtual city by investing finite resources—which later became integrated into many urban studies curricula. SimCity and its progeny are delightfully open-ended, permitting a myriad of possibilities and outcomes. As the historian Kevin Baker shows, SimCity embeds some very questionable assumptions—for instance, that growth is the primary measure of success, or that regulation generally dampens economic activity. Apparently, the game designer, Will Wright, had been reading the controversial work of conservative urban theorist Jay Forrester and designed these ideas into the mechanism of his popular title.[20]

It is hard to overstate how much thought and effort goes into designing today's digital experiences. Social media, ride-sharing, and other apps employ teams of people with letters after their names to meticulously shape and refine what consumers see, do, and feel. Algorithms carefully curate content. User testing is constant. Just as casinos and grocery stories think very carefully about layout—hiding signals that time is passing or stocking the sugary cereal at eye level for a child—so do digital spaces aim to maximize sales or engagement through design. The difference being that mediated environments like websites are endlessly reconfigurable and adapt in real-time to individual or collective consumer behaviors. To paraphrase Heraclitus, you never enter the same digital environment twice.

The power to shape consumer experience has long been abused by companies trying to maximize profits. Unsubscribing to a service has always been harder than subscribing. The box indicating permission to sell your data to third parties has long been faint in color and prechecked. It didn't take online retailers like Amazon long to begin to experiment with changing their prices for individual consumers based on what they know about them, as Jonathan Zittrain documented in 2009.[21] Yet, the FTC held its first workshop on the topic of so-called dark patterns—design decisions aimed at exploiting the limitations of consumers—in 2021. The best explanation for this delay in recognizing the potential of design to exploit the mediated consumer is technological incapacity: regulators were unable to see the hidden will of companies in the digital systems they use every day.

Danielle Citron and others interrogate the ways automating state and federal agency decision-making undermines guarantees of due process and fair rule-making procedures by obscuring changes to how rules are interpreted and applied without opportunity for notice, comment, or meaningful

challenge.[22] Indeed, the American legal system permits lawmakers to confer legislative authority upon agencies due to agency expertise and discretion. As Citron and I argue, automating the administrative state undermines its very legitimacy by redelegating that agency expertise and discretion to engineers and machines.[23]

Yet another salient example involves the embedding of gender, race, class, and other biases in machines. In the prescient 1996 article *Bias in Computer Systems*, Batya Friedman and Helen Nissenbaum use airline reservation systems and other case studies to show how "biases in computer systems can be difficult to identify let alone remedy because of the way the technology engages and extenuates them."[24] After developing a framework that delineates the problem of bias in computer systems, the authors discuss strategies for identifying and mitigating bias and unfairness.

While the community discussed Friedman and Nissenbaum's insight at the time, decades would pass before bias in computer systems entered the mainstream, largely due to the work of women and minority activists, artists, and scholars. Safiya Noble explored the biased assumptions of search engines in 2012.[25] A 2017 paper by Aylin Caliskan, Joanna Bryson, and Arvind Narayanan reveals how unfairness and discrimination become embedded in language models used to translate text—as when, for example, translating gender-neutral sentences back and forth between English and Turkish introduced the gendered pronouns "he" and "her" to accompany the words "doctor" and "nurse," respectively.[26] Contemporaneous work showed gender and race or skin color disparity in the accuracy of facial recognition systems. A 2018 paper by Joy Buolamwini and Timnit Gebru found that three commercial gender classification algorithms available at the time performed worse for women and people with darker skin color and worse still for "darker females," that is, that intersectionality further amplified bias.[27]

Such work eventually received sustained recognition by the press and other visible institutions like TED and the Aspen Institute. Popular titles also helped shepherd these ideas into the mainstream. The 2016 book *Weapons of Math Destruction*, by Cathy O'Neil, traces how embedded assumptions and errors in the algorithms behind a range of consequential decisions—from lending to insurance to civil engagement—reify societal discrimination and exacerbate income inequality.[28] Noble's 2018 *Algorithms of Oppression* builds on her early work challenging the neutrality of search engines and other information-sorting algorithms. She concludes that self-serving, monopolistic practices by search providers lead to biased systems that privilege

cis-men and white people.[29] And in *Race After Technology*, Ruha Benjamin evidences the way automation generally reproduces historic race and gender hierarchy while enjoying a pretense of inclusion and objectivity.[30]

Often the culprit is not, or not only, a resource-constrained official, greedy corporation, or neglectful engineer. It is *all of us*—the biased society that produced the data upon which algorithmic models are based. It is the very logic of sorting people into categories by reference to measurable attributes, which, as Crawford explores in *Atlas of AI*, far predates computing.[31]

Arguably, the extensive, contemporary attention heaped upon manipulation and bias in digital systems is evidence that law and technology recognizes hidden will after all. Setting aside that few of the scholars mentioned earlier in the chapter are law professors or lawyers, there were decades during which systems were manipulative and biased, and few were publishing on the topic. More importantly, there have been almost no changes to law and legal institutions to address these issues, despite the growing attention. We are only beginning to see regulatory interest as of this writing, with federal agencies arguing that existing law already grants them the authority to pursue abuses.

I don't know when you are reading this book. But I can safely assume that digital mediation has only deepened. The widespread dissemination of augmented or virtual reality, discussed in Chapter Four, as well as ambient computing embedded in human environments, holds the potential to shape the perceptions, experiences, and behaviors of people at all times. Regardless, the core insight remains the same: the law and its students struggle to see the full range of responsible actors within sociotechnical systems. Technology makes a shell game of responsibility in any era however the shells change. This technological incapacity, in turn, skews accountability and prevents, or delays by decades, intervention.

Ungovernability

The important book *Privacy's Blueprint* by law and communications scholar Woodrow Hartzog begins with the premise that "design is everything."[32] Hartzog's thesis is that policymakers should require values such as privacy and security to be designed into digital consumer products and services; but they seldom do. Technology's unique characteristics suggest why. Academics and policymakers alike tend to accept the present configuration of emerging technology as inevitable, and often fail to uncover the many hidden choices

behind everyday artifacts and systems. As a consequence, legal analyses of technology are at best incomplete. Law and technology analysis overlook both how design could be different, and who might be responsible for technological harm.

Yet these concerns are in a sense mere minions to the archenemy of clear thinking about law and technology: the idea that technology cannot be governed. It is hard to overstate the influence of this fatalistic myth in undermining law's role.

The idea that technology is ungovernable wears many clothes. In the early days of cyberlaw, a number of scholars and activists argued that the internet was *literally* impossible to rule. Lessig opens *Code* with a quote from a Grateful Dead lyricist who co-founded a prominent digital rights organization. "Governments of the Industrial World, you weary giants of flesh and steel," intones John Parry Barlow. "You have no sovereignty where we gather." Less poetically, academics and others questioned how governments could possibly regulate activities occurring outside their physical borders without cutting themselves off from the rest the global economy. Lessig wrote *Code* in large part to evidence the prospect and danger of greater government and industrial control over digital environments.

Turns out the internet can be regulated. Indeed, the claim that any given technology, by its very nature, cannot be reached by human laws is implausible. Technology nevertheless enjoys a veneer of ungovernability, bolstered by a series of intuitive, but ultimately specious, arguments. The first is that contemporary and emerging technology is too complex or "technical" for lawyers to understand or address. Recall Judge Easterbrook's pronouncement from the introduction that legal scholars won't be winning the (nonexistent) Nobel Prizes for computer science anytime soon. If courts and policymakers, like academics, cannot understand the technology, they stand little chance of regulating it wisely.

This perception finds support in the many high-profile instances where jurists or policymakers disavow knowledge of technology or, worse yet, declare themselves incapable of understanding it. In 2022, University of Washington law professor Eric Schnapper argued a case with potentially enormous consequences for the internet before the Supreme Court. The case turned on whether internet platforms like YouTube could be liable for aiding and abetting terrorism on the basis that an algorithm recommended terrorist recruitment videos to vulnerable youth. At oral argument, Justice Elena Kagan could have been Judge Easterbrook addressing the inaugural

cyberlaw conference. "We're a court," she reminded my colleague. "We really don't know about these things. You know, these are not like the nine greatest experts on the internet."[33]

Justice Kagan was proposing that Congress, not the Supreme Court, should determine the scope of Section 230—the federal law at issue, which immunizes internet platforms for much of the content people post there. But Congress has scarcely a better reputation for technical acumen. In 2006, Senator Ted Stevens of Alaska—at the time, the longest-serving Republican Senator in history—described the internet as "a series of tubes." The questions Senators asked Facebook founder Mark Zuckerberg during a 2018 hearing on social media are the stuff of lore and ridicule.[34] Questions at the hearing included how social media makes money without charging consumers to access it ("Senator, we run ads.") and whether ads for chocolate a Senator had recently seen online were based on the company somehow overhearing his oral comments at the first day of the hearing ("No.").

The conclusion of this book discusses the steps that could be taken to address shortfalls of technical expertise. Restoring funding to the Office of Technology Assessment, for example, which advised Congress on technology for twenty years until it was defunded in the 1990s, would be a good start. Regardless, the idea that technology is too complex for legal minds is belied by areas of law—such as patent—that often turn on precise technical understandings. A core competency of lawyers, after all, is learning a context well enough to argue about it. The argument that the inner workings of technology are too complex for law professors or practitioners to understand proves too much. People are complicated, too. Financial systems are very complicated, but a hands-off approach to regulating financial markets can be disastrous. Complexity is endemic to human affairs; it cannot foreclose regulation all on its own.

Another commonplace argument against governability is not that technology is too complicated to understand, but that it moves too fast. Here is the logic of this position: Like the lie that travels halfway around the globe while the truth is putting on its shoes, technology advances and iterates so quickly that law cannot hope to catch up. By the time lawmakers and courts—sclerotic almost by design—get around to addressing a new technology, that technology has already evolved to the point where intervention is moot or ill-advised.

The belief that technology—and technology alone—invariably outpaces law is widespread. It is also demonstrably wrong. Technology is hardly

unique in its capacity for vertiginous change. Recall Willie Stark's 1946 remark in *All the King's Men* from the introduction: "The law is always too short and too tight for growing humankind. The best you can do is do something . . . and by the time the law gets on the books you would have done something different." Norms around drinking, drugs, labor, divorce, race, and myriad other social facts, have changed rapidly in ways that required equally rapid legal responses.

1938 saw the passage of the Fair Labor Standards Act, as millions of women entered the U.S. workforce for the first time amidst the labor shortages of World War II. Just a few years later, those same women were displaced by new laws—the Selective Training and Services Act of 1940 in particular—that required employers to fire them in favor of returning male veterans. The introduction discusses how, in the 1920s, the United States *passed a constitutional amendment*—by design, an arduous legal process with many steps and participants—outlawing the sale and consumption of alcohol in response to a growing temperance movement. A dozen years later, this same prohibition was repealed by constitutional amendment, having led to economic malaise and the rise of organized crime. Following a century of criminalization, marijuana went from being almost completely outlawed in every state in 2011, to being legal recreationally in most states, in just over a decade. Meanwhile, pursuant to the Controlled Substance Act, the Drug Enforcement Agency regularly adds new chemical compounds to its list of outlawed or restricted drugs.

There are plenty of examples of law responding rapidly to technological change as well. The USSR launched the first satellite into outer space in 1957. Congress created NASA in 1958. A mere five years later, the United Nations adopted legal principles governing the exploration and use of outer space, which became the basis for the 1967 Outer Space Treaty. Later, agreements governed orbital weaponry, moon rights, and the formation of the International Space Station. Rockets travel at five miles a second. Somehow the law kept up just fine.

Partially in response to the 1983 movie WarGames,[35] in which a young Matthew Broderick nearly starts a nuclear war by hacking into a Department of Defense computer, Congress passed the Computer Fraud and Abuse Act (CFAA) of 1986. The law has its flaws. It has been misused to threaten computer science researchers and critiqued as overbroad. The CFAA is also beginning to show its age at the time of this writing in light of AI. Yet, the law managed to articulate a credible anti-hacking standard for over thirty years.

The idea that technology moves too fast for law to respond is specious. A more subtle account posits that even if law as an institution could keep pace with technology, it shouldn't. Because the rules will seldom be wise.

The subtler concern that law will get technology wrong—often called the problem of "pacing"—grows out of the work of David Collingridge. Embedded in the Technology Policy Unit at the University of Aston in Birmingham in the 1970s, Collingridge wrote *The Social Control of Technology* to describe what he saw as the central problem for law and technology. His 1980 book posits that regulators hoping to channel technology in the public interest face a "double-bind" of information and power. Information because the usage and consequences of technology cannot be determined in advance. Technological artifacts and systems must permeate society before their impacts can be understood. Power because once technology is distributed far and long enough for its impacts to be grasped, people become invested in it to the point that it is difficult to reign in or regulate.[36]

There is much truth to the so-called Collingridge dilemma. Chapter Two delves deeper into STS, which contends that technology both shapes, and is shaped by, social and societal dynamics. STS resists technological determinism, that is, the idea that technology will follow an invariable path or have wholly predictable consequences. Rather, technology's impact on society will play out over time in accordance with cultural, social, economic, and other forces. STS supports Collingridge's argument that knowledge about the impact of technology will never be perfect, and that technology will land against the backdrop of existing structures of power.

The pacing problem is, nevertheless, dramatically overstated. First, many of the adverse consequences of technology can be, and indeed are, predicted. I am astonished anew every time I think about the way the United States began licensing the construction of nuclear power plants in the 1950s without a clear plan to dispose of nuclear waste. There was no official policy on this well-understood problem until 1982, and nuclear waste disposal remains an unsolved problem as of this writing. The attitude seemed to be: "Well, we split the atom after all. How hard could this little problem of radioactive material be?"

Early scholars repeatedly warned of the adverse consequences of social media. Warnings about privacy by Daniel Solove[37] or cyber-stalking and hate speech by Danielle Keats Citron and Mary Anne Franks[38] were largely ignored by industry and government until they couldn't be. The user experience designer Harry Brignull coined the term "dark patterns" to describe deceptive or misleading interfaces in 2010, over a decade before the FTC

brought its first dark pattern actions. Today, it is widely understood that AI embeds societal bias.

Just as the *advantages* of emerging technology can be anticipated—for why else would a technology deserve investment and protection?—many of the adverse consequences of emerging technology can be anticipated as well. A later chapter on methodology discusses some of the techniques of envisioning and forecasting that can improve the government's and society's capacity to anticipate and channel technological impacts. Regardless, the pacing problem need not lead to regulatory paralysis even under imperfect information. It does not follow that governments must stay their hand unless or until the trajectory and impact of technology are completely understood.

As lawyers know, the law has many mechanisms for addressing uncertain or changing circumstances. These include a choice between rules—which are specific and inflexible—and standards. The CFAA's longevity is a product of defining hacking as "unauthorized access" or "exceeding authorization," relatively amorphous standards that can evolve with the times. The FTC has emerged as the leading enforcement agency in the technology sector, in part because of its broad mandate to police against "unfair and deceptive practices."

Even detailed rules can be amended. Various laws, from national surveillance to digital copyright, have built-in sunset provisions or other requirements to periodically revisit the state of technology or society. And then there's federalism. Local jurisdictions can take differing approaches to new technologies, from bans or heavy regulation to benign neglect. This allows for regulatory experimentation and limits the geographic impact of poor choices. Increasingly, officials in the United States and Europe are experimenting with "regulatory sandboxes," wherein new techniques or technologies can be deployed in a limited setting without having to comply with burdensome regulations.[39]

In short, the pacing problem offers a false dichotomy between forestalling and flubbing legal intervention. Regulation has always been what political and economic theorist Charles Lindblom called a "science of mudding through."[40] We expect regulators to act with imperfect information and iterate in response to social facts on the ground. Law is among the few forces society has by which to channel technology in the direction of human flourishing. The pacing problem provides comfort only to libertarians, hopeless techno-optimists, or the people who stand to profit from a technological Wild West.

Innovation Fetishism and Charismatic Technology

The argument that technology is too complex or moves too fast paced for law to regulate it takes place against a particular backdrop: the belief that hampering technological progress risks societal well-being. Such "innovation fetishism," to borrow a term, posits that no nation can afford to stand in the way of technological progress.[41] Technology improves human standards of living. Technology confers America's primary economic advantage; hampering innovation would mean falling behind in the global economy. And not just health or economics are at stake. Technology appears central to state intelligence and military advantage, such that the regulation of technology, even when there are known downsides, could threaten national security.[42]

The favored boogeyman of innovation fetishism is the so-called precautionary principle. This approach to governance, which dates back at least to German environmental policy of the 1970s, would ban or limit potentially dangerous new scientific techniques or technologies until they can be proven safe. Critics of precaution posit that the approach does far more harm than good—in the words of one prominent commentator, the precautionary principle "costs lives"[43]—because the gains of scientific or technological advance tend vastly to outweigh the costs. If and when a new technology causes harm, society can take steps to mitigate it. Until then, the proper ecosystem for government to cultivate is "permissionless innovation."[44]

As I've argued elsewhere, the evidentiary basis for the claim that the precaution principle impedes progress is curiously thin. This can be seen in the paucity of examples furnished by critics of precaution. Were technophobia-fueled precaution so prevalent and dangerous, one might suppose there would be many examples of its ills, expanding year by year. The number of examples in the literature has, if anything, dwindled. Critics of precaution still cite nuclear power as a road not taken in clean energy and continue to lament the slow start of genetically modified organisms (GMOs) due to unfounded public concerns—though both nuclear power and GMOs are widespread. Recent evidence of toxicity has taken the shine off of a third favorite example, the internet, and the prospect of regulation of AI seems too far off to serve as a replacement. Two or three bedtime stories are not enough to keep frightening the children.

One reason there are so few examples of the precautionary principle impeding progress, at least in the United States, is that bans on science and

technology are vanishingly rare. At the turn of the millennium, President George W. Bush signed an executive order impeding stem cell research by prohibiting federal funding for new stem cell lines. Even this policy, which President Barack Obama soon overturned, never prohibited stem cell research per se. Indeed, the labs working with existing stem cell lines continued to apply for and receive National Institute of Health funding. A handful of cities recently banned facial recognition by the police; the bans proved temporary. Perhaps the closest we can come to categorical bans on technology are chemical and biological weapons conventions. Unfortunately, these bans were not precautionary; many people died horrible deaths before the Biological Weapons Convention in 1972 and the Chemical Weapons Convention in 1992.

There is another side to this coin. Not only are American and other societies overly solicitous of technical innovation, but our institutions also tend to look the other way when technology fails. This wasn't always the case. Few ignored the Titanic or Hindenburg. But in our collective, contemporary desire to understand technology as constantly improving in furtherance of human wellbeing, we show a remarkable aptitude to ignore evidence to the contrary.

A wonderful paper turned book by information scientist Morgan Ames develops a theory of "charismatic technology," artifacts and systems so captivating that their "utopian promises . . . persist even when the technology does not deliver."[45] Her lead example is One Laptop per Child—the ill-fated MIT Media Lab effort to overhaul global education by disseminating rugged, open-source "XO laptops" to children in under-resourced nations. Despite lavish investment by individuals and giant tech companies, appearances at TED or Davos, and endless positive press coverage, One Laptop per Child was a dismal failure. The XO laptops were never cheap, functional, or resilient enough to make economic sense. More importantly, the entire premise of the effort was based on privileged Western notions of learning through experimentation and play. Yet the proponents of One Laptop per Child continued to tout the effort long after evidence showed it wasn't improving educational outcomes.

Recent events furnish another example. Among the most important tools to try to contain the novel coronavirus (COVID-19) has been effective contact-tracing, that is, figuring out who has had contact with an infected person so they can test and isolate as well. Historically, contact-tracing has been done by people. Health authorities interview the positive case to

determine who else may have been exposed and collect their contact information for a follow-up. It's a time-consuming, sometimes invasive process, but critical to slowing the spread of the virus.

An admirable impulse to help out during the COVID-19 crisis led technologists all over the world to independently develop a means by which to try to automate the process of contact-tracing. Most zeroed in on the Bluetooth capability of mobile phones, which allows wireless speakers and other kinds of devices in close proximity to connect to mobile phones without an auxiliary cable. So-called contact-tracing apps kept an anonymous log of nearby phones, and should someone report testing positive for COVID-19, the app notified anyone who had been in sufficiently close proximity for long enough that they risked exposure.

It is easy to see the intuitive appeal of contact-tracing apps. All you need is a Bluetooth-enabled mobile phone and suddenly you can protect yourself and others from exposure. Turns out contact-tracing apps did not work any better than XO laptops. Hindsight is 20/20, but in retrospect, the problems were obvious. Despite reassurances of anonymity and privacy, relatively few people downloaded them. Proponents and apologists for contact-tracing apps—which involved time, effort, and *millions* of emergency dollars that could have been used another way—would later blame the failure on limited participation. In reality, the problems ran far deeper.

The most obvious flaw was the potential for false positives and negatives. Bluetooth travels through walls and protective gear, COVID-19 does not. The apps would alert safe people in the neighboring apartment or vehicle of exposure. To determine how much exposure warranted notification, health authorities had to set a one-time threshold upon deployment of the app—typically six feet for at least fifteen minutes. Even were these very rough estimates valid at the time when the app was developed, COVID-19 famously mutated to become more and more contagious. All of this assumes, meanwhile, that contagious people were using the app. False positives meant needless tests or quarantines; false negatives gave infected, often asymptomatic people a mistaken sense of reassurance.

As with other charismatic artifacts and systems, developers and some health authorities continued to tout contact-tracing apps as an important measure to address the spread of COVID-19 well into the pandemic. Proponents of the technology cherry-picked results, often written up by the very technologists who developed contact-tracing apps, purported to show the intervention saved thousands of lives. But these papers were based on

statistical estimates with few controls. Yes, some set of COVID-19 positive people got tested because of a notification. But that same result would obtain from *randomly* notifying citizens of exposure. The failures of contact-tracing apps have yet to be fully acknowledged. When acknowledged at all, they are blamed on people's supposedly misplaced privacy fears.[46]

Such is often the case with technology. Society is asked to get out of technology's way. And, if the technology doesn't get to where it's going, society is supposed to pretend it never passed by.

Technological Exceptionalism, Revisited

Over the years, scholars in various disciplines have bristled against "technological exceptionalism," the idea that technology is somehow unique from other social or societal phenomena. I have come to roughly the same conclusion, with an important caveat: technology is not so different from other social facts, but it sure *feels* different. And this perception of difference can have deep consequences for legal analysis and intervention.

The idea that new technology "changes everything" is seductive. We are all aware of advances—often medical—that have altered life expectancy or quality of life in dramatic ways. The effect of emerging technology on the individual and collective psyche, however, is often broader than technology's tangible or material impact. I invoked Leo Marx in the beginning of this chapter. In his 1964 book *The Machine in the Garden*, Marx coined the term "technological sublime" to refer to the almost spiritual feeling new technology invokes in the observer.[47] But the strongest feeling societies tend to associate with technological development is change. And change spells opportunity.

Change lets you pretend something is new. The term regulatory entrepreneurship, coined by law professors Elizabeth Pollman and Jordan Barry, refers to "pursuing a line of business in which changing the law is a significant part of the business plan."[48] It is different from, but related to, traditional regulatory arbitrage in which businesses exploit gaps in the law or differences across jurisdictions. Uber "disrupts" transportation by connecting "independent" drivers to consumers through an algorithmically managed app. Airbnb disrupts the hospitality industry by turning in-law suites into hotel rooms. Neither company complies with the full set of labor, safety, and other regulations that attend these sectors.

Obviously, were Uber and Airbnb to start taxi and hotels businesses without complying with the law, they would be shut down. And eventually these companies did draw regulatory scrutiny. What they needed was time to operate long enough to show their convenience, and especially to build up a constituency of consumers and workers who relied upon their services and would help them advocate for more permissive rules. The argument that they were *technology* providers, not taxis or hotels, furnished Uber and Airbnb with a veneer of plausible deniability that they were flouting the law.

Not only does technology provide cover for flouting rules long enough to gain a foothold, but shifts in technology can also supply politicians and judges with a reason to reopen settled legal issues. "Technological change occupies a unique place in the modern development of judicial doctrine," write communications scholar Monroe Price and law professor John Duffy, "because it provides a singularly uncontroversial justification for modifying established doctrine."[49]

In the mid 1990s, in work largely forgotten or overlooked by law and technology as a field, Price and Duffy use examples from cable television and the internet to show that lawmakers and courts react opportunistically to changes in telecommunications and media to advance an existing worldview. "Technological changes play a part in the evolution [of law]," Price and Duffy write, "but . . . not so powerful a role as legislators claim in justification of the statute that has emerged." Meanwhile, doctrinal transformations justified by technological advancement "have more to do with jurisprudential reforms otherwise favored by the Justices, than with actual shifts in the structure or organization of telecommunications" (id. at 980).

Particularly visible changes to technology justify change to the political, economic, or cultural status quo, or in its retrenchment. This insight is hardly lost on scholars of technology and race. Legal scholars such as Ifeoma Ajunwa, Jessica Eaglin, and Pauline Kim explore the tendency of law and technology to frame questions as narrowly technological, overlooking the social and cultural backdrop.[50] Hence, society expects firms to de-bias technical systems such as hiring or sentencing algorithms, rather than acknowledging the racist overtones of employment and criminal law. Other scholars of technology and race evidence how law and policy help to obscure the ways emerging technology reinforces racial and other inequities.[51]

Technological change depends on the observer. When the observer is a judge or policymaker, new technology has just as much potential to entrench power as to displace it.

Law and technology in theory and practice has yet to fully grapple with the tendency of objects and systems to daunt and confuse. Technology feels inevitable rather than contingent. Digital and physical artifacts and systems obscure will, agency, and responsibility. And technology radiates a fatalistic sense of ungovernability. At the same time, technology is offered as evidence of changed circumstances, reopening social, economic, and political debates under the guise of the new. Technology resists restraint, while placing law and norms in a constant state of defense.

The remainder of this book discusses how the field of law and technology can rise to the challenge with greater consistency. Chapter Two distinguishes law from other disciplines, such as the philosophy of technology and STS, by reference to law's normative and pragmatic orientation. Law is comfortable with prescription, and expert in the levers of power needed to channel technology in the public interest. The chapters that follow argue for a methodical approach to law and technology, aimed at overcoming technological incapacity and lending coherence to the field. Only by approaching technology with adequate rigor and care can the field of law and technology—and the rule of law generally—hope to bring technology in line with societal values.

Notes

1. Leo Marx, *"Technology": The Emergence of a Hazardous Concept*, 64 Soc. Res. 965 (1997).
2. Kate Crawford, Atlas of AI: Power, Politics, and the Planetary Costs of Artificial Intelligence (Yale University Press 2021).
3. Madeleine Clare Elish, *Moral Crumple Zones: Cautionary Tales in Human-Robot Interaction*, 5 Engaging Sci., Tech., & Soc'y 40 (2019).
4. Herbert A. Simon, The Sciences of the Artificial (MIT Press 1968).
5. Jacques Ellul, The Technological Society (Vintage Books 1964) (1954).
6. Ruha Benjamin, Race After Technology: Abolitionist Tools for the New Jim Code (Polity Press 2019).
7. Frederick Ferré, Philosophy of Technology (University of Georgia Press 1995) (1988).
8. Bruno Latour, *Technology is Society Made Durable*, 38 Soc. Rev. 103 (1990).
9. *E.g.*, Ariel Ezrachi & Maurice E. Stucke, Virtual Competition: The Promise and Perils of the Algorithm-Driven Economy (Harvard University Press 2016).
10. In 2015, Senator Wyden (D-OR) introduced a bill targeting "mobile aerial-view device," defined broadly to encompass "any device that through flight or aerial lift obtains a dynamic, aerial view of property, persons or their effects." While S. 1595 still excludes some concerning technologies, the bill wisely broadens beyond the FAA definition to address the privacy concerns that arise through the affordances of robotic surveillance.
11. Orin S. Kerr, *An Equilibrium Adjustment Theory of the Fourth Amendment*, 125 Harv. L. Rev. 476 (2011).
12. The reference is to Eugene Volokh, who in 1995 envisioned people would access digital music files through "public music vending machines." Others of Volokh's predictions about the technology proved eerily accurate. Germinal work such as *Cheap Speech and What It Will Do* generally focused on the format and movement of speech, rather than its content. Eugene Volokh, *Cheap Speech and What It Will Do*, 104 Yale L.J. 1805 (1995).

13. STEVEN JOHNSON, EMERGENCE: THE CONNECTED LIVES OF ANTS, BRAINS, CITIES, AND SOFTWARE (Scribner 2001).
14. Langdon Winner, *Do Artifacts Have Politics?* 109 DAEDALUS 121 (1980).
15. Winner cites to Robert A. Caro's biography of Moses, which some have contested.
16. LAWRENCE LESSIG, CODE AND OTHER LAWS OF CYBERSPACE (Basic Books 1999); Joel R. Reidenberg, *Lex Informatica: The Formulation of Information Policy Rules through Technology*, 76 TEX. L. REV. 553 (1997).
17. Where some see "algorithms of oppression" (Safiya Umoja Noble) or "weapons of math destruction" (Cathy O'Neil), others see "equality engines" (Orly Lobel) or the opportunity to "accelerate democracy" (John McGinnis).
18. David C. Vladeck, *Machines Without Principals: Liability Rules and Artificial Intelligence*, 89 WASH. L. REV. 117 (2014).
19. Madeleine Clare Elish, *Moral Crumple Zones: Cautionary Tales in Human-Robot Interaction*, 5 ENGAGING SCI., TECH., & SOC'Y 40 (2019).
20. Kevin T. Baker, *Model Metropolis*, LOGIC(S) (Jan. 1, 2019), https://logicmag.io/play/model-metropolis/.
21. JONATHAN ZITTRAIN, THE FUTURE OF THE INTERNET AND HOW TO STOP IT (Yale University Press 2008).
22. Danielle Keats Citron, *Technological Due Process*, 85 WASH. U. L. REV. 1249 (2008).
23. Ryan Calo & Danielle Keats Citron, *The Automated Administrative State: A Crisis of Legitimacy*, 70 EMORY L.J. 797 (2021).
24. Batya Friedman & Helen Nissenbaum, *Bias in Computer Systems*, 14 ACM TRANSACTIONS ON INFORMATION SYSTEMS 330 (1996).
25. Safiya Umoja Noble, *Missed Connections: What Search Engines Say About Women*, Bitch Magazine (Spring 2012).
26. Aylin Caliskan, Joanna J. Bryson, & Arvind Narayanan, *Semantics Derived Automatically from Language Corpora Necessarily Contain Human Biases*, 356 SCIENCE 183 (2017).
27. Joy Buolamwini & Timnit Gebru, *Gender Shades: Intersectional Accuracy Disparities in Commercial Gender Classification*, 81 PROC. OF MACH. LEARNING RSCH. 77 (2018).
28. CATHY O'NEIL, WEAPONS OF MATH DESTRUCTION: HOW BIG DATA INCREASES INEQUALITY AND THREATENS DEMOCRACY (Crown 2016).
29. SAFIYA UMOJA NOBLE, ALGORITHMS OF OPPRESSION: HOW SEARCH ENGINES REINFORCE RACISM (New York University Press 2018).
30. RUHA BENJAMIN, RACE AFTER TECHNOLOGY: ABOLITIONIST TOOLS FOR THE NEW JIM CODE (Polity Press 2019).
31. KATE CRAWFORD, ATLAS OF AI: POWER, POLITICS, AND THE PLANETARY COSTS OF ARTIFICIAL INTELLIGENCE (Yale University Press 2021). *See also* FREDERICK SCHAUER, PROFILES, PROBABILITIES, AND STEREOTYPES (Harvard University Press 2003).
32. WOODROW HARTZOG, PRIVACY'S BLUEPRINT: THE BATTLE TO CONTROL THE DESIGN OF NEW TECHNOLOGIES (Harvard University Press 2018).
33. Ariane de Vogue, *What Is the Future of the Internet? Don't Ask the Supreme Court*, CNN (Feb. 21, 2023, 6:02 PM EST), https://www.cnn.com/2023/02/21/politics/future-of-internet-supreme-court-analysis/index.html.
34. *See, e.g.*, SPORTZ! (@SportzByRyan), X (Apr. 10, 2018) ("Mr. Zuckerberg. . . hypothetically if someone's VCR won't stop flashing 12:00, how would you suggest they fix that?").
35. WARGAMES (Metro-Goldwyn-Mayer Pictures 1983).
36. DAVID COLLINGRIDGE, THE SOCIAL CONTROL OF TECHNOLOGY (Cambridge University Press 1980).
37. Daniel J. Solove, *"I've Got Nothing to Hide" and Other Misunderstandings of Privacy*, 44 SAN DIEGO L. REV. 745 (2007).
38. Danielle Keats Citron, *Cyber Civil Rights*, 89 BU LAW REV. 61 (2009); Danielle Keats Citron, *Law's Expressive Value in Combating Cyber Gender Harassment*, 108 MICH. L. REV. 37 (2009); DANIELLE KEATS CITRON, HATE CRIMES IN CYBERSPACE (2014); Danielle Citron & Helen Norton, *Intermediaries and Hate Speech: Fostering Digital Citizenship for our Information Age*, 91 BU L. REV. 1435 (2011); Mary Anne Franks, *Unwilling Avatars: Idealism and Discrimination in Cyberspace*, 20 COLUM. J. GENDER & L. 224 (2011); Mary Anne Franks, *Sexual Harassment 2.0*, 71 MD. L. REV. 655 (2012).

39. Institute for Reforming Government, Removing Barriers to Innovation: How Regulatory Sandboxes Can Solve Kitchen Table Issues (2024), https://reforminggovernment.org/wp-content/uploads/2024/05/IRG_SandboxReport.pdf.
40. Charles E. Lindblom, *The Science of "Muddling Through,"* 19 Pub. Admin. Rev. 79 (1959).
41. Marko Ampuja, *The New Spirit of Capitalism, Innovation Fetishism and New Information and Communication Technologies*, 23 J. Eur. Inst. for Commc'n & Culture 19 (2016).
42. Policymakers and academics sometimes repeat self-serving, evidence-free claims by industry that regulating AI cedes our international edge to rivalrous nations such as China. The reality is more complicated.
43. Adam Thierer, Permissionless Innovation: The Continuing Case for Comprehensive Technological Freedom (Mercatus Center George Mason University 2016) (2014).
44. *Id.*
45. Morgan G. Ames, *Charismatic Technology*, 1 Critical Alts. 12 (2015).
46. U.S. Gov't Accountability Off., GAO-20-666SP, Science, Technology Assessment, and Analytics: Science and Tech Spotlight, Contact Tracing Apps (2020).
47. Leo Marx, The Machine in the Garden: Technology and the Pastoral Ideal in America (Oxford University Press 2000) (1964).
48. Elizabeth Pollman & Jordan M. Barry, *Regulatory Entrepreneurship*, 90 S. Cal. L. Rev. 383 (2017).
49. John Duffy & Monroe Price, *Technological Change and Doctrinal Persistence: Telecommunications Reform in Congress and the Court*, 97 Col. L. Rev. 976 (1997).
50. Ifeoma Ajunwa, *Artificial Intelligence, Afrofuturism, and Economic Justice*, 112 Geo. L.J. 1267 (2024); Jessica M. Eaglin, *When Critical Race Theory Enters the Law & Technology Frame*, 26 Mich. J. Race & Law 151 (2021); Pauline Kim, *Manipulating Opportunity*, 106 Va. L. Rev. 867 (2020).
51. Safiya Umoja Noble, Algorithms of Oppression: How Search Engines Reinforce Racism (New York University Press 2018); Ruha Benjamin, Race After Technology: Abolitionist Tools for the New Jim Code (Polity Press 2019).

Suggested Readings

Morgan G. Ames, *Charismatic Technology*, 1 Critical Alts. 12 (2015).

Jessica M. Eaglin, *When Critical Race Theory Enters the Law & Technology Frame*, 26 Mich. J. Race & Law 151 (2021).

Bruno Latour, *Technology Is Society Made Durable*, 38 Socio. Rev. 103 (1990).

Leo Marx, *"echnology": The Emergence of a Hazardous Concept*, 64 Soc. Res. 965 (1997).

Langdon Winner, *Do Artifacts Have Politics?* 109 Daedalus 121 (1980).

TWO
THE SCALE AND THE REACTOR

Introduction

The popular 2020 documentary *The Social Dilemma* features a Silicon Valley engineer-turned-technology critic named Tristan Harris. Prompted to distinguish the ills of social media, Harris looks directly into the camera and observes: "No one got upset when bicycles showed up. Right?"[1]

The moment makes for good television. But it is not, in fact, right. The introduction of the bicycle at the turn of the nineteenth century elicited an uproar in Europe and the United States, running the gamut from public safety to shifting gender roles. Like many technologies, from social networks to shopping carts, bicycles underwent a complex cultural negotiation before coming to rest, for now, on banality. Harris is not an academic. He can be excused for not reading, say, the complete works of Trevor Pinch. Yet, little effort is needed to find similarly dubious claims about the interplay between technology and society in the pages of law reviews and other academic journals. There are at least the several I have made over the years.

Law professors and lawyers don't always get technology "right." My concern is not that jurists possess a poor understanding of the inner workings of technology itself. You will find few echoes of Frank Easterbrook here. While it is true that law professors interested in computers never did "win a Nobel Prize . . . for advances in computer science," law and technology professors, in general, have proven adept at understanding and explaining how the technology they are writing about actually works. It's part of our training. What we, and many others, fail to appreciate most often is the *context* in which technology operates.

Chapter One describes some of the specific ways technology tends to daunt and confuse observers, which has consequences for legal analysis and policymaking. As it happens, there exist entire areas of study aimed at providing greater nuance around the interplay between technology and society. The philosophy of technology dates back at least to Ancient Greece.

Law and Technology. Ryan Calo, Oxford University Press. © Ryan Calo 2025.
DOI: 10.1093/9780197526170.003.0003

Democritus, Heraclitus, Plato, and Aristotle all espoused views about "technê"—roughly, the useful application of knowledge. Later philosophers explored the nature of technology as well: its relation to culture (Jacques Ellul), morality (Shannon Vallor), how society is structured (Lewis Mumford), metaphysics (Martin Heidegger), and the human condition (Hannah Arendt).

This chapter—titled after the *Whale and the Reactor* by Langdon Winner[2]—focuses on a decades-old area of study called science and technology studies (STS). The multidisciplinary field of STS specifically explores how social, cultural, and other forces shape technology, and how, in turn, technology shapes people and society. STS is, in many ways, the antidote to technological incapacity. STS scholars document technology's contingency, trace the role of human responsibility in technical systems, and warn against the allure of emerging technology and its "hazardous" consequences.

STS is devoted to getting technology right. This chapter argues that STS is indispensable to law professors and other jurists interested in an accurate understanding of technology and its interplay with law. Simply put, STS helps law and technology scholars avoid oversimplification and error, which is indispensable for law to channel technology wisely. This chapter summarizes STS for the legal academics and policymakers, pointing out the enormous utility of its central insights for the legal analysis of technology. Yet, there are also important limits to relying on STS. STS and law are engaged in fundamentally different projects. A second part of the chapter distinguishes law and technology from STS by reference to the unique concerns—normativity and pragmatism—that characterize law as a discipline.

The many longstanding insights of STS are critical to navigating the complex social fact of technology. And the legal academy is catching on. A number of law and technology scholars already usefully deploy STS in ways that deepen legal knowledge, and several of the most prominent contemporary STS scholars come to the field with legal or policy training. Others invoke the insights and language of STS without necessarily realizing they are doing so.

That legal academics are turning to STS is a positive development. STS anticipates and deepens any number of core law and technology insights. Before Joel Reidenberg's *Lex Informatica* or Lawrence Lessig's *Code*, there were Langdon Winner's insights about the bridges to Long Island and Bruno Latour's commentary on the heavy hotel key and seatbelt alarm.[3] Before Jonathan Zittrain's insights on the Internet's generativity, there was Ivan Illich's notion of conviviality.[4] Today, privacy and cyberlaw discourse

benefits immensely from the STS-inflected insights of contemporary legal scholars such as Lisa Austin, Julie Cohen, Mireille Hildebrandt, Woodrow Hartzog, Lyria Bennett Moses, Deirdre Mulligan, Paul Ohm, Paul Schwartz, Ari Waldman, and many others. It would benefit, too, from greater engagement with Pinch, Latour, Winner, Sheila Jasanoff, Robert McGinn, John Law, and other preeminent STS scholars.

Yet, the embrace of STS is "positive" in a second sense as well. STS, generally, and the popular method of social constructivism, in particular, tends to be scrupulous in its avoidance of normativity. STS is less interested in what is morally just than in what is socially accurate. This is true even of the critical turn in STS, which, while foregrounding politics, identity, and distributions of power, commonly falls short of offering a full-throated normative account capable of justifying state intervention. Meanwhile, nearly all of the emphasis STS places on the sheer complexity of sociotechnical systems tends to trip up pragmatic efforts at reform. STS can be so nuanced and multivalent that implementing its insights in the form of tangible law and policy is daunting, amounting often to the recommendation that technology's political dimensions should be more legible, and more people should participate in their development. STS is beautiful music, but can you dance to it?

Law is different. It has to be. Law and technology has its own burgeoning tradition, one characterized by a normative and practical commitment to safeguarding rights and interests in the face of technological change and to promoting human flourishing. Two aspects distinguish law's approach from STS and other fields that study the social and societal aspects of technology. The first is *normativity*. Legal scholars are relatively adept at moving between the "ought" (normative) and the "is" (descriptive). As academics go, we law professors truck in normativity to a degree second only to moral philosophy. Most law review articles move seamlessly from describing a problem to prescribing a solution that best meets the goals of individuals, groups, and society.

This normativity follows, for many, from the nature of law itself. To paraphrase Max Weber in *Politics as a Vocation*, law claims a monopoly on the legitimate use of violence.[5] The passage and interpretation of laws have tangible effects on people and communities within their ambit. Breaking the law ostensibly justifies a response by the state that can involve taking away liberty, property, and even life by force. As Ronald Dworkin, Robert Cover, Robin West, and other legal scholars argue persuasively, legal claims are moral claims in other guise.[6]

The second unique facet of law—and, by extension, law and technology—is *practicality*. Law as a field possesses a certain "relentless pragmatism," as Julie Cohen has called it,[7] calling to mind a pragmatic tradition handed down to us most famously by Oliver Wendell Holmes Jr. We are ready—nay, delighted—to describe the levers of power in detail and to endorse solutions to the problems we identify. Legal academics expect to say what society should do and how it ought to do so. In this sense, at least, the scale has something to teach the reactor.

What Is STS?

In recent years, I have immersed myself in the STS literature. The field is rich, provocative, and challenging, to summarize. Work in STS spans decades, continents, and disciplines; its concepts are disparate and intricate. There is not even consensus around what the acronym stands for—science and technology studies, or science, technology, and society.

At its core, STS is concerned with studying science and technology as observable social phenomena. Drawing from history, sociology, anthropology, philosophy, and other disciplines, STS seeks to understand how science and technology are developed, by whom, and to what societal ends and effects. STS is particularly associated with close study of specific contexts—or "techno-social systems"—with the aim of interrogating how science and technology shapes, and is shaped by, societies and cultures in which they are embedded.

The field is also challenging to contextualize historically. Some would locate the origins of STS in the 1930s work of historians, sociologists, and philosophers like Lewis Mumford, Robert Merton, or Ludwik Fleck. Nearly all of the early STS scholars hail from these disciplines. Others would trace STS to the 1960s, and especially to *The Structure of Scientific Revolutions*, of "paradigm shift" fame, given Thomas Kuhn's emphasis on studying science as a social enterprise.[8] Still others would date the origins of STS to the establishment of the science, technology, and society initiatives that grew up at some American universities (namely, Stony Brook, Cornell, and MIT) in the late 1960s in reaction to perceived misuse of science and technology in medicine and war. Or later still, to the field's embrace of social constructivism and rejection of the idea that technology acts on society in predictable or inevitable ways. It was these later scholars—such as Pinch and Winner—who

begin to tie the project of uncovering the social nature of technology to a well-functioning democracy.

Regardless of when it began, STS has coalesced into a mature, multivalent area of study. Several generations of scholars identify themselves as working in the field, and multiple universities across the world, including my own, have STS departments or centers as of this writing.

Intellectually, there is convergence within STS around the basic idea that science, technology, or "techno-science" together consist of socially embedded phenomena susceptible to study. STS scholarship diverges with respect to the nature of that phenomena and how best to interrogate it, a divergence that plays out both at the level of subject matter and methodology. In addition to resisting the notion that technology is somehow separate from the rest of society, most STS scholars embrace the use of case study. "If you want to understand STS," writes John Law, "you need to read through its cases."[9] Yet, under this tent dwell many different approaches, objects of study, and concepts.

One way to organize the field is to borrow Robert McGinn, Sheila Jasanoff, and others' dichotomy between an internalist and externalist perspective.[10] The internalist looks at the nature and practice of science and technology. The internalist asks who "does" technology, within what institutional settings, and under what pressures and constraints. Here, the object of study is the content of the original "black box," the site of design and engineering itself. While quantitative methods are available—some follow Merton, the sociologist of science, in measuring scientific output and influence numerically—most internalist STS is decidedly qualitative. As in *Laboratory Life*, Bruno Latour and Steve Woolgar's influential book about scientific practice at the Salk Institute,[11] or in Michel Callon's discussion of the science of scallops as a social system,[12] researchers approach the site of scientific or technological production in the posture of anthropologists or ethnographers, observing and unpacking the practice of science or engineering itself.

If internalist scholarship explores the social processes behind technology, externalist scholarship explores technology's interaction with society at large. This research involves the way technology shapes the social realm and is shaped in turn—acknowledging, of course, that considerable overlap exists in the demand for technology, the development of technology, and the interaction of technology with societies in which it is embedded. The externalist may look, for example, at the (ahem, notably contentious) introduction of the bicycle into nineteenth-century London. Or, the externalist may

compare the "sociotechnical imaginaries" that shape American and South Korean approaches to nuclear power.[13] Such work involves a broad range of social science, from history to sociology and religion, to political science and law, and to gender, race, and other critical theory.

Thus, as Jasanoff summarizes, "STS combines two strands of work dealing, respectively, with the nature and practices of science and technology [] and the relationship between science, technology, and society."[14]

STS in both traditions has generated innumerable insights about technology over the years. Among the most enduring is the challenge to technological determinism—the idea that technology follows a specific trajectory and perforce acts upon society in predictable ways. Determinism is a stubbornly intuitive concept, often deployed rhetorically, according to Sally Wyatt, by politicians and industry to provide cover for extractive, often harmful, activities.[15] (Law professors will immediately recognize Wyatt's argument in evergreen industrial and political talk of "innovation.") Most STS scholars resist hard determinism as self-interested fantasy. Both the development and adoption of technology is contingent, they argue, resting upon, but also informing, the societal context in which it emerges. For many STS scholars, the very line between technology and society is a social construct, perhaps even a "hazardous" one, as Leo Marx has argued.

Closely related to determinism, but arguably distinct, are the concepts of technological autonomy and technological essentialism. Technological autonomy refers to the capacity of technology to exert or propagate sociocultural influence without further human intervention. Technological essentialism understands technology to possess specific qualities that distinguish it from other kinds of social facts, or from previous or constituent technology. Deterministic claims often accompany claims of technological autonomy and essentialism, but determinism does not logically entail either.

While most every STS scholar would acknowledge that the path of technology cannot be fully anticipated in advance, and that the impacts of technology on society depend on the ways humans and institutions understand and use their tools, the field diverges from there. Scholars in the social constructivist tradition eschew determinism to emphasize the mutual, social shaping of technology. Social construction of technology (SCOT) scholars perceive arbitrariness in the very distinction between the social and the technical, relying instead on close study of the myriad ways technology participates alongside other social dynamics in constituting social

reality. Case studies in social construction tend to be meticulous and messy, and the methodology emphasizes the need for "interpretive flexibility" when approaching the significance of technology. Technology has no fixed meaning but varies by observer and by context, and changes over time.

Other social constructivists emphasize materiality, the "thingness" of technology. They look for the role artifacts play in fixing and stabilizing social relations, that is, the ways technology renders society more durable. For adherents to actor network theory (ANT), objects themselves possess a form of agency—the theory places human and nonhuman "actants" on similar footing, with neither claiming epistemological priority in the social environment. Despite this form of technological autonomy, many adherents to ANT nevertheless continue to foreground the role of human agency, using the method to show how agency, power, and norms get distributed across a system through embodiment in artifacts.

STS rejects determinism, and yet it doesn't too. The idea that technological choices shape people in particular ways rests, paradoxically, at the heart of mainstream STS. Indeed, many people outside the field associate STS with Langdon Winner's assertion that "artifacts have politics." Whether by design or accident, or some mixture, technologies embed certain expectations and constraints. Artifacts have affordances or, more accurately, artifacts have the capacity to alter human affordance in specific ways. Their design can enable, limit, or prevent behavior. For Winner, a low bridge, like the ones designed by Robert Moses, can encode race and class into urban architecture. An automated tomato harvester can prioritize firmness over taste, affecting the genetic makeup of the tomatoes available at a supermarket. For Latour, technological change can substitute for social discipline, as when a heavy hotel key substitutes for disciplining guests for failing to leave their room keys with the clerk, or when a spring mechanism substitutes for disciplining individuals for failing to close their doors behind them.

Just as individual artifacts have politics, so too can large techno-social systems take on, in STS historian Thomas Hughes's words, a certain technological momentum.[16] Norms and law may shape the early days of the automobile, but eventually car culture takes on a life of its own. Other systems rely upon and demand particular forms of governance. A nuclear reactor—let alone a nuclear warhead—implies an authoritarian bureaucracy to a greater extent than a windmill farm. Some technologies possess a quality of "conviviality"—a kind of open-endedness—that renders them more democratic and autonomy enhancing.[17] None of these claims amount to a full-throated

defense of technological determinism, autonomy, or essentialism. But nor are they in another universe.

For many years now, "critical" STS scholars have looked at the disciplining or political nature of technology through the lens of identity and power. Discussions of capitalism and class arose with the earliest examinations of technology and society, which were grounded in a Marxist tradition that carries on to this day. Feminist conceptions of technology date back to at least the 1970s and have undergone several overlapping shifts in emphasis. Early feminist scholars of technology sought to dismantle the purportedly biological basis for associating technology with maleness. "An initial challenge for feminists," writes Judy Wajcman, "was to demonstrate that the enduring identification between technology and manliness is not inherent in biological sex difference."[18] Rather, technology had been—and often still is—defined by reference to industrial and military pursuits where men predominate, even though women were often the first to work with technology when it was less attractive, like early computers.[19] Women were excluded from the technical realm or required to sacrifice gendered identity upon entry as soon as the technical realm seemed profitable. Everyday artifacts used mostly by women, from the sewing machine to the shopping cart, were in turn excluded from the world of the technical.[20]

These early explorations tended to see technology as neutral, if exclusionary. In dialogue with mainstream STS, feminist discourse in the 1980s began to unpack the myriad ways technology itself is political and gendered, part of a sociotechnical process of entrenching gender hierarchies. Artifacts have politics—those of men. Gender relations, like other social relations, are "materialized" in artifacts. By the 1990s, and in parallel with critical studies in law and elsewhere, these scholars began to destabilize the very notion of gender as a viable construct. As early as 1985, with the publication of Donna Haraway's *Manifesto for Cyborgs: Science, Technology, and Socialist Feminism*,[21] scholars, artists, and activists also began to explore how the blurring of boundaries between the human and the machine afforded new feminist narratives or "imaginaries," that is, the opportunity to challenge and revisit societal notions of identity.

Related themes of exclusion, mediation, and power appear throughout critical STS. Scholars of race and technology have documented the longstanding role of artifacts and systems in policing racial hierarchy. Simone Browne draws parallels between the eighteenth-century lantern laws—rules requiring unaccompanied non-White people traveling at night

to carry a source of light—and contemporary biometric surveillance of minorities.[22] Safiya Noble exposes how search technology presented Black girls as pornographic while white girls were presented as angelic and pure.[23] Ruha Benjamin explores how software and algorithms reify race and racism, while, in Benjamin's words, "appearing to be neutral or benevolent when compared to the racism of the previous era."[24] Lisa Nakamura envisions the global internet as a continuation of Western imperialism by other means.[25]

In parallel to techno-feminists, many critical STS scholars resist "narratives of victimization"[26] that cast its subjects as the inevitable victims of technology. Charlton McIlwain traces the role of computers in racial subjugation—with the story of IBM's "Book of Life," for example, which was used to identify and track Black South Africans in the 1960s.[27] But McIlwain takes equal care to excavate Black agency in computing, namely, the significant role of African Americans in designing and defining technology since the 1970s. While some STS scholars of race (like André Brock) are dubious of utopian narratives, others see Afrofuturism as an opportunity to reveal the contingent and contestable nature of associations between race and technology.[28] The editors of the popular STS volume *Technicolor: Race, Technology, and Everyday Life* acknowledge the role of technology in racial subjugation while self-consciously "mov[ing] beyond the binary logic that insists that race and technology are always at odds."[29]

Critical STS is rich and various, encompassing a wide range of experiences and identities as well as their intersection. Techno-feminism has long explored the many intersections between gender and "other axes of power such as race, colonialism, sexuality, disability, and class."[30] American and European universities have active Queer and intersectional STS working groups. Whereas Browne's *Dark Matters* focuses on the "surveillance of blackness,"[31] Toby Beauchamp's *Going Stealth: Transgender Politics and U.S. Surveillance Practices* traces the role of state surveillance in enforcing gender conformity.[32] Yet more work explores the ways technology mediates disability, including, for example, the reductive role of machine learning in categorizing people with autism.

Critical STS shares an internal commitment to foregrounding asymmetries of power, past and present. Critical STS also aligns with the broader STS community in understanding technology as a social phenomenon susceptible to study, and especially in revealing artifacts as embedding (gendered, racialized, and ableist) politics. As Safiya Noble puts it: "the more we can make transparent the political dimensions of technology, the more we

might be able to intervene."[33] For critical STS, as for social constructivism, technology plays an important role in constituting material and social reality. Critical STS places a greater emphasis on power and identity and tends to evince a more visible commitment to specific values such as feminism, socialism, and antiracism. But alongside certain bespoke interventions, such as racial literacy and bias auditing, critical STS joins the broader STS community in its core diagnosis: society needs greater transparency regarding the political dimension of technology and more diverse participation in its design, development, and adoption.

In sum, technology is both the product of social forces and a shaper of social activity. The trajectory of technology is therefore contingent upon the complex interplay between people and things. At the same time, artifacts alter human affordances and channel behavior, and those affordances can reflect, intentionally or not, the politics of those artifacts' designers. When you open up the black box, you find that technology, like soylent green, is made out of people. The politics of artifacts are not arbitrary—they reflect societal norms and expectations, including capitalism, colonialism, patriarchy, and bigotry. But nor are they inevitable. Greater awareness of these logics and biases, greater and more diverse participation in technology at all levels, and better storytelling about the role of technology in society can bend our tools toward conviviality and human flourishing—a decidedly lawyerly-like normative pursuit.

Much more could be said about the field of STS. I have left out many insights, critiques, and disciplinary twists and turns. We could speak of coproduction, of relevant social groups, of boundary objects, and of the distinction between High and Low Church. We could compare and contrast STS with philosophers of technology from Habermas to Ellul. My purpose, for now, is to showcase for the law and technology reader just how much water there is under the bridge.

Ignorance Is Less and Less a Defense

Most American law and technology scholarship to date does not draw upon STS—at least not explicitly. The Introduction mentions *Channeling Technology Through Law*, the 1973 tour-de-force in which Laurence Tribe describes the blueprint for the now defunct Office of Technology Assessment. *Channeling Technology Through Law* includes a short

discussion of the purposes and methods of technological assessment—the process by which regulators gain an understanding of the risks and benefits of emerging technology—and an even shorter discussion of considerations for how best to structure federal institutions to channel technology. The vast majority of Tribe's book is devoted to examining specific technologies such as supersonic transport through the lens of cost-benefit analysis. While *Channeling Technology Through Law* does not self-consciously leverage STS, which had yet to cohere as a field, it embraces the STS method of case study and gesturing toward the iterative, two-way nature of social and technological interaction. Technology assessment is the road not taken in law and technology. "Even when it has consumed government resources," writes Lyria Bennett Moses, "technology assessment has received little attention from lawyers. With few exceptions, legal scholarship and technology assessment literature do not intersect."[34] Yet, with some notable exceptions explored in this chapter, law and technology scholarship has been largely silent on STS to date.

This silence is strange. Law and society scholars rely on the insights of anthropologists and sociologists (and indeed have doctorates or training in those fields along with law). The law and literature tradition draws heavily from literary theory, where the commonality seems to be that both law and literature are written down and involve imagination. There is still less connective tissue to the highly influential law and economics movement, where the purported disciplinary overlap between law and economics is the very thesis of the field: What if law were about Kaldor-Hicks efficiency? You would think that a discipline devoted to the study of law and technology would draw deeply and expressly from a field possessing decades of knowledge about technology as a social fact. It doesn't.

The silence has costs. The lack of awareness of STS among legal scholars writing about technology has unfortunate consequences. One consequence is that we do not benefit from the wisdom of scholars who have covered roughly the same ground. It would be too strong to say that law and technology reinvents the wheel. Legal scholars deploy insights about technology in particular ways, for particular purposes. And we shouldn't be surprised that good ideas find analogs in earlier disciplines. But law and technology has been sounding similar notes to STS for years without listening to and learning from its music.

Examples abound. The idea that physical and digital architecture amount to behavioral constraints akin to rules—that "code is law"—is a bedrock

principle of the influential field of cyberlaw. Closely associated with law professor Lawrence Lessig, the notion that software and other technical constraints can regulate conduct to a greater degree than even law remains a perennial subject of discussion in law and technology. Then and now, the debate would benefit from core insights of STS. As Julie Cohen has noted, "[t]he insight that artifacts constrain ('regulate') behavior has a long history within STS, and it is mined within that literature in far [more] subtle ways."[35]

Winner opens his 1980 article *Do Artifacts Have Politics?* with the same example as Lessig two decades later: Robert Moses's low bridges to the suburbs, designed to deter public buses coming from New York City. Winner offers several more case studies, from nuclear fission to the tomato harvester, meant to illustrate other, more subtle ways—sometimes unintentional or structural—that technology shapes society. Winner is interested in the way architecture can regulate but also in the way technologies assume and necessitate certain organizational structures (nuclear fission and hierarchical bureaucracy) or demand conformance from their environment (the tomato harvester and firmer, less flavorful tomatoes).

Bruno Latour's discussion of European hotel keys, designed to be bulky to discourage patrons from taking them off site only to lose them, starts from the premise that design can channel behavior. "If [guests] conform to the manager's wishes," writes Latour in 1990, "it is not because they read the sign, nor because they are particularly well-mannered. It is because they cannot do otherwise."[36] Elsewhere, (in 1992) Latour described a repetitive, high pitch alarm that sounded when he failed to buckle his seatbelt. After resisting for some time, Latour relented: "I was at peace with the law," writes Latour, "I wished to break it but I could not." Adding, with a flourish that Lessig and Oliver Wendell Holmes Jr. would have both appreciated, "I cannot be bad anymore."[37]

Yet, the idea that "technology is society made durable" is about much more than regulation by architecture. Latour is interested in the way that design changes behavior and the reasons why people delegate discipline to objects. He is also interested in the broader role of objects—keys, cameras, seatbelts, doors, and many others—in fixing and stabilizing social relations. What is interesting to Latour is the manner in which moral choice becomes distributed and fixed across people and things. Objects become a kind of "dark matter," invisibly holding together our social and moral universe. Yet, law and technology scholars generally follow Lessig in treating architecture as just another "modality of regulation," albeit less visible than law or amenable

to resistance, rather than as a powerful societal force that can shape and fix social relations.

The very debate that sparked cyberlaw as a field—over the degree of control that was possible in networked environments—would have benefited from greater interpretive flexibility. In the internet's early days, a handful of scholars and activists begin to envision the technology as a distinct and separate community from the physical world. They spoke of the internet as "cyberspace," a concept previously associated with science fiction and Danish visual art. Some understood cyberspace as a libertarian haven, free from state control. The theory was that because the internet was everywhere and nowhere, cyberspace would be impossible to regulate because no sovereign could enforce its rules.

A rejoinder to techno-libertarian utopian thinking came swift on its heels. Scholars argued that governments and other powerful institutions would find ways to reassert control, even in cyberspace. That's where the idea that code is law came to prominence. In his 1999 book *Code and Other Laws of Cyberspace* and in prior writings, Lessig anticipated that the mediated nature of the internet risked even more exquisite control over people than written law, as sovereign powers and firms and institutions within their boundaries came to appreciate the ways in which code itself can constrain and channel behavior. States could direct their coercive powers at the very design of networks and interfaces, changing the rules by changing the Internet's architecture.

Others began to push the pendulum back in the other direction, arguing that Lessig had overstated the potential of code to regulate. In the influential 2008 book *The Future of the Internet (And How to Stop It)*, Jonathan Zittrain, too, worries that powerful forces, state and corporate, would come to dominate us through technology. Yet, Zittrain opens his chapter on "Perfect Enforcement" with a cheerful observation: "So far Lessig's worries have not come to pass." Somehow the malleability of code had yet to yield to sovereign power in the way Lessig feared.

Why didn't Lessig's prophecy come to pass? Zittrain coined the term "generativity" to describe an apparently intrinsic quality of internet architecture that stacked the deck in favor of people. A generative technology is open-ended and malleable in a way that fosters creativity and, by some mechanism, hampers domination. "A system's level of generativity," writes Zittrain, "can change the direction of the power flow between sovereign and subject in favor of the subject." Only by deliberately reducing the internet's

generativity, that is, altering its essential architecture, could powerful actors reassert total control.

As with Lessig, Zittrain would have benefited from greater engagement with the STS debate over determinism, especially Thomas Hughes's specific theory of "momentum," that is, "the propensity of technologies to develop previously defined trajectories unless or until deflected by some powerful external force." The notion of generativity at the heart of Zittrain's book also calls to mind earlier STS insights. Generativity is a kind of essential quality of openness that some technologies possess and others do not. Generative technologies foster creativity and resist domination. The five factors that make a technology generative are "(1) how extensively a system or technology leverages a set of possible tasks; (2) how well it can be adapted to a range of tasks; (3) how easily new contributors can master it; (4) how accessible it is to those ready and able to build on it; and (5) how transferable any changes are to others—including (and perhaps especially) nonexperts."

Students of STS may recognize an affinity to Ivan Illich's concept of "conviviality" from his 1973 book *Tools for Conviviality*: "Tools foster conviviality to the extent to which they can be easily used, by anybody, as often or as seldom as desired, for the accomplishment of a purpose chosen by the user. The use of such tools by one person does not restrain another from using them equally. They do not require previous certification of the user. Their existence does not impose any obligation to use them. They allow the user to express his meaning in action."[38] Illich goes on to describe the role of law in recovering conviviality, which in turn acts as a safeguard against domination. Though the concepts differ in significant ways, it is regretful that Zittrain did not see himself to be in dialogue with Illich, in that both men are gifted scholars concerned with the relationship between open-ended tools, governance, and human flourishing.

Other legal scholars came to the same conclusion as Zittrain, but for different reasons. Tim Wu's *When Code Isn't Law*, for example, shifts attention away from the regulator who targets software as means or modality of regulation, and toward the savvy coder who understands software as a vehicle by which to exploit and influence legal obligations without the exposure and costs of lobbying for legal change.[39] For Wu, Jack Goldsmith, and others, code could just as easily be a mechanism of legal avoidance as control.[40] James Grimmelmann argues similarly that the "plasticity" of software sets code apart from other architectural interventions into behavior, opening possibilities for adaptation and resistance.[41]

Summing up this journey in 2015, law professor Jack Balkin reads like an STS scholar in the sociological tradition:

> The features that are most salient about our technology may depend on how people come to use it. Often people use technology in ways its designers did not foresee or intend. That is especially so for what Jonathan Zittrain calls "generative" technologies, which offer multiple sites and possibilities for innovation. What seems particularly important and salient about technology changes over time as people work with and through new technology. Moreover, technology, like law, mediates social relations between human beings—including relations of power and control. Because those relations are always evolving, our assessment of what is most interesting or worrisome about a technology may change too.[42]

Said another way, cyberlaw took decades to wind up where STS would have started.

Privacy law scholars have long observed the importance of metaphor and analogy in driving legal outcomes regarding technology. According to Michael Froomkin, the level of protection courts will afford encryption turns on which metaphor for encryption most appeal to judges: is encryption more like a car that transports information, a safe that hides secrets, or a house in which conversation takes place? Noting that "ideas are weapons," Froomkin urges defenders of civil liberties to analogize encryption to a kind of language, and hence a form of speech.[43] Daniel Solove argues that reliance on George Orwell's *1984* as a metaphor for contemporary privacy problems undermines the foundations of privacy law by failing to capture the harm. Solove urges scholars and policymakers to invoke Aldous Huxley's *Brave New World* and Kafka's *The Trial* instead.[44]

STS is interested at least as deeply in the interplay between imagination, technology, and policy. Writing initially about nuclear power in the United States and South Korea, Jasanoff and Sang-Hyun Kim develop the concept of sociotechnical imaginaries to explore how different cultures conceptualize the role of particular technologies, which in turn drives their respective policy choices.[45] Wyatt, Leo Marx, and others show how narratives of technological progress legitimize industry prerogatives through "justificatory determinism."[46] Myths and rituals accompany technology in an effort to enhance its political impact, only to be resisted and appropriated in a process Bryan Pfaffenberger refers to as a "technological drama" in three

acts.[47] Critical STS, like critical race theory, also frequently touches upon the role of narrative, from the "black secret technology" of Ben William's deindustrialized Detroit music scene[48] to the "teddy bear patriarchy" of Donna Haraway's natural history museum.[49]

A lack of familiarity with STS limits legal scholarship by withholding wisdom and nuance. A second unfortunate consequence is that many scholars of law and technology fall into some of the very traps STS grew up to avoid.

I mentioned Orin Kerr's influential theory of the Fourth Amendment, which holds that new technology upsets the balance between the capacities of law enforcement and criminals, leading judges to reinterpret the Constitution in an effort to restore the status quo through a process of "equilibrium adjustment."[50] STS would see this claim as strongly deterministic, observing that the development and use of new technology arises from the same societal dynamics that shape the decisions of law enforcement, jurists, and Holmesian bad men. STS would not understand technology to operate in isolation from other social phenomena. While the invention of the motor vehicle may have changed the affordances of bootleggers, an equally plausible candidate for the tectonic shift in our understanding of the Fourth Amendment in the early twentieth century is the sudden obligation to stop millions of Americans from drinking. Technological change becomes, if anything, an expedient to justify a cultural sea change in the relative power of state and citizen.

What Law Brings

It is an open secret that law professors operate at a kind of trade deficit with other disciplines: we import concepts and methods at a far greater rate than we export them. In our exuberance for new frameworks, sometimes we apply ideas from other disciplines without acknowledging that those ideas are contested or outdated in their discourse of origin. When I say legal scholars should leverage STS, I do not mean to say that STS is a singular field that law can simply apply. Rather, STS is a set of methods, concepts, and assumptions—a way of seeing technology as social fact—that I think of as indispensable to the study of law and technology.

Notwithstanding an overall dearth of attention to method, many in the legal academy have turned to quantitative, qualitative, and historical social

science in the wake of legal realism to study law as a societal phenomenon. The same could occur, indeed is occurring, with respect to technology, especially in intellectual property and innovation where empirical scholarship is complicating deterministic views around incentives to create and build. Law itself can be understood as a sociotechnical system, as Mireille Hildebrandt, Joshua Fairfield, and others suggest, or at least a component of the "social" that comprises any given technical, social system.[51] Could not law and technology come to be seen as the legal branch of STS—or, if one prefers, the technology studies wing of law and society?

Law and technology are different sorts of social facts. To understand one is not to understand the other. STS could tell you quite a bit about the shopping cart as a social phenomenon—its history, the values it embeds, how shopping carts changed the experience of shopping, and how those experiences translated into website design when shopping migrated online. But STS can't tell you whether taking the last box of cereal out of a stranger's shopping cart in a store before anyone has paid constitutes theft. STS can explain how the term "jeep" went from referring to new Army recruits to referring to a certain kind of lightweight military vehicle; STS can explore how car companies rebranded the jeep into the Jeep, touching off of latent demand for the "sports utility vehicle." But neither STS, nor any other field of inquiry but law, can account for whether a rule reading "no vehicles in the park" justly applies to a World War II memorial jeep set on a pedestal to commemorate veterans.[52]

I believe a working knowledge of STS is critical to law and technology scholarship. STS presages some of law and technology's core insights and can help avoid the pitfalls and errors that attend technology as social fact. My own work draws heavily from STS in defining technology and assessing technology's impact on human affordances.

I now make a second claim, however, arguably in tension with the first: powerful as these tools are, legal scholars hoping to rely upon STS methods and insights will encounter significant limits. More than this, importing STS wholesale into law and technology has the potential to undermine what is unique about our field.

We have different knowledge, of course. I hope I don't offend, and doubt that I surprise readers, in observing that the typical STS scholar is not as proficient at legal analysis as the typical law professor. Reading through otherwise masterful treatments of technology and society, one can stumble across any number of discussions of law that feel lightweight or inaccurate

in much the same way as law and technology scholarship can be lightweight and inaccurate about technology—for example, STS contains idiosyncratic ideas about products liability, information privacy, outdated-when-written notions of the regulatory state, and Panglossian assumptions about the power of legal reform.

That STS doesn't always get law exactly right is unsurprising, but also superficial. Several prominent STS scholars have law degrees—they understand law very well. The content of the law can be learned, with enough diligence and care, by anyone. I teach a hundred or so people law myself every year. Latour wrote an entire book about law.[53] Legal scholars and STS scholars also team up and write together, a prospect Easterbrook overlooked when he warned cyberlaw scholars away from discussing technology. There are many ways to bring greater sophistication and accuracy to the role of law in sociotechnical systems. If the concern is expertise alone, I see no valid reason why law and technology could not fold neatly into STS, particularly the field's external orientation (Science, Technology, and Society), focused as it is on the role technology plays in society.

There are at least two limits to STS for law and technology, however, which bring with them two opportunities for law as a field to share back with STS. The first is the law's comfort with normativity, second in academia only to moral philosophy. The law does—perhaps must—truck in normativity to a far greater degree than STS. The second is law's pragmatism, and especially the facility of legal scholarship to navigate levers of power. Legal scholarship lays out what to do about the problems it identifies, and how to do it. These are general qualities of legal scholars, but especially true of law and technology. While there is plenty of legal scholarship that is positivist or empirical, law and technology as a field leans heavily toward a normative agenda: the use of one powerful social force, law, to channel another.

Law's Normativity

Normative is a word with several senses. Normative can simply mean "of or pertaining to norms," that is, observable societal expectations. It is possible to observe, for instance, that adding some version of the word "please" to requests is a social norm in many cultures, without necessarily commenting on the propriety or wisdom of politeness. Law and technology scholars are well aware of norms in this sense, in part due to Lessig's popularization of the

way social norms, like architecture and markets, serve as one "modality" of regulation.[54] Affect norms, and you affect behavior. STS is, if anything, more attendant to norms of this kind than law and technology is to date. Norms play a big role in shaping technology, and in technology's role in shaping culture.

A more commonplace understanding of normative in legal circles is as a synonym for prescriptive, in the sense of making recommendations about the world instead of, or in addition to, describing it. Most legal scholarship, including law and technology, is normative in this basic sense, concluding with a recommendation to change law or technology in order to address the problem the author has diagnosed. The practice is so commonplace that legal scholars sometimes refer to "part three" arguments as shorthand for a paper's recommended course of action, reflecting the way other disciplines refer to "reviewer number two" as shorthand for harsh critique. As Richard Delgado reminds us, "the normative orientation remains the unspoken mode of legal analysis and scholarship," for better or for worse.[55]

A prescription must have a basis; every "should" invites a "why." Which brings me to the final, thickest sense of normative. Laws are normative insofar as law, which demands obedience on pain of violence, must be justified morally. Some readers may be familiar with Robert Cover's memorable opening line in *Violence and the Word*: "Legal interpretation takes place on a field of pain and death."[56] An unfavorable legal interpretation can translate into the loss of property, liberty, and even life—deprivations that not only invite, but demand, normative justification. Other readers may be familiar with Ronald Dworkin's famous argument regarding law as integrity: law is inexorably linked to normativity insofar as legal interpretation involves placing prior precedent in the best moral light.[57] The obligation to interpret existing "institutional legal materials" against a coherent set of principles—justice, fairness, and due process—follows, for Dworkin as for Cover, from the necessity of justifying coercion by the state.[58]

In a memorable reply to Judge Richard Posner's 1997 lecture, *The Problematics of Moral and Legal Theory*,[59] the philosopher Martha Nussbaum describes the relationship between normativity and law with characteristic force and clarity. Posner denies the potential for moral philosophical insights to channel behavior and practice, and hence he sees a limited utility for law and legal theory. Normative ethics is all well and good to debate but it doesn't change anything, Posner argues. Nussbaum responds

to this claim by tracing dozens of examples, from the influence of John Locke on the Constitution to the work of Immanuel Kant on international law, where the impact seems undeniable. Ultimately, Nussbaum sees a symbiosis between normative theory and law. Jurists "needed a theory to give their work direction by providing an account of the ethical core of their enterprise," she writes. But just as lawyers and legal scholars needed Kant, so "Kant also needed these entrepreneurs in order for his ideas to have practical impact."[60]

If law is normative in this way, then legal scholarship in the prescriptive tradition must be normative as well—a position Robin West defends convincingly and at length over several writings (sometimes with coauthor Danielle Keats Citron).[61] For West, the aim of normative legal scholarship "is to make the law better, rather than to explain or describe subtle or nonobvious features of law or the legal system.... Legal scholarship is and should be about what justice requires. It therefore must be normative."[62] If Dworkin is right, and stating what the law is "requires an interpretive act that itself rests on some cluster of stated or unstated moral principles,"[63] then even describing the law has a normative component. But surely, articulating what the law ought to say does.

I doubt very much that West, Dworkin, Cover, or Nussbaum would require that all legal scholarship be normative in one sense or another. There is quite clearly a place for descriptive or positivist legal discourse, formally committed to the rigorous advancement of knowledge and little else. Yet, while it is possible to write about the legal aspects of technology without prescription, that is not the tradition. Law review articles and books by law and technology scholars overwhelmingly conclude on a prescriptive note and often on a moral basis. *Oughts* and *shoulds* abound.

This tendency holds even for law and technology scholars who see "norm" as a synonym for societal expectation, such that influencing norms becomes another avenue for, or modality of, regulation. It is, again, possible to observe the social fact of a norm without commenting on its propriety. But when this instrumental conception of normativity gets deployed in law and technology, it generally does so in furtherance of an exogenous goal. When Zittrain argues that "code-backed norms"[64] should play a role in improving consumer privacy, he is making two sorts of claims. The first is that it is possible to use technology to change societal norms around information sharing in a way that enhances privacy. The second is that this is a good idea. He is

saying, in essence, that we ought to make people feel like they should respect privacy.

In contrast to law, the vast majority of STS is no more normative than the methods of the humanities from which it draws. Like sociology or anthropology, STS is focused on describing a particular facet of the world: how technology is shaped by, and in turn shapes, society. Though, of course, total objectivity is impossible, the study of technology as a social phenomenon requires a certain detachment. The social constructivist tradition, in particular, with its emphasis on interpretive flexibility (multiple perspectives that iterate over time), resists even the idea that technological contexts remain stable, let alone take on objectively moral characteristics.

None of this is lost on the field. Winner challenges these very tendencies in technology study in his memorable 1993 essay, *Upon Opening the Black Box and Finding It Empty*.[65] His read of social constructivism, like my own, suggests that announcing a "theoretical or practical position on technology and human well-being . . . seems forbidden on methodological grounds." For Winner, "interpretive flexibility soon becomes moral and political indifference." Winner calls upon STS to move away from pure social science and "offer coherent arguments about which ends, principles, and conditions deserve not only our attention, but our commitment."[66]

At a 2004 lecture at Stanford University, Latour also laments social constructivists critiques of science, including his own, albeit on a different basis: science has a social element, but critique has gone too far in "comparing the laws of physics to the rules of baseball." Critique did not open a black box and find it empty so much as "witness[] the black box of science remain closed and that it was rather the tools that lay in the dust of our workshops, disjointed and broken."[67]

Winner and Latour direct their remarks at the more inward social constructivist tradition. Is the same true of other areas of STS? In researching this book, I have spoken to a number of contemporary STS scholars about their field. When I pose the question about normativity, these scholars tend either to confirm that STS is about generating knowledge, not opining on right and wrong, or else point to the work of a critical STS scholar like Donna Haraway. Haraway, Benjamin, Nakamura, Noble, Beauchamp and other critical scholars of technology invoke concepts, such as antiracism, anticolonialism, and gender liberation, that are strongly entangled with normative values such as equality, plurality, and dignity. It is clear these scholars do not like the politics they see in many artifacts. For that matter, neither do I.

Yet, one seldom finds in such discussion a full-throated defense of legal intervention on the basis of an articulated normative theory. In her book *Normative Jurisprudence*, West writes:

> *Critical legal theorists, since the 1970s, have asked probing questions about the relationship of law to power. . . . What is the relation of law, some critical theorists ask, to patriarchal power, or, others ask, to the power of capital, or, still others, to white hegemony, or, recently, to heteronormativity? . . . These are all good questions, but their answers do not imply anything one way or the other about the goodness or badness of the law so unmasked. . . . Rather, the focus of the contemporary critical theorist is relentlessly limited to the relationship of law to the power that perverts, produces, or constrains it, or alternatively, to the social cultural, or political power that is legitimated and mystified by the hegemony that is law's product.*[68]

For West, critical scholars—she is looking at critical legal studies—are not necessarily interested in normativity in the same way as Cover or Dworkin. Rather, critical scholars in this tradition are interested in surfacing hidden sources of domination and power and explaining doctrines and institutions on their basis. Critical legal theorists, including of race, gender, and other forms of identity, underscore the ways law protects and legitimates asymmetries of power, without necessarily developing a normative baseline by which to assess these phenomena for purposes of justifying state intervention—of which, indeed, they are understandably suspicious. The same can be said of much STS literature in the critical tradition.

Law's Pragmatism

Let us assume, however, that at least some work in STS is inherently normative. That normativity can struggle to find real world purchase. STS prescriptions tend to lack anything like the specificity of STS diagnoses. The contrast can be jarring, akin to seeing a doctor who explains your condition to you in great detail and finishes by admonishing you to "live healthier." STS remedies tend to take the form of broad commitments to unmasking the politics of artifacts and systems and encouraging greater and more diverse participation in technological development. The field features intricate discussions of problems with relatively little attention devoted to the

precise changes to people, institutions, or society the author would like to see. Where specific changes are delineated, they are (quite understandably) seldom accompanied by a working knowledge of the levers of power that might see them enacted into policy in practice.

Some see the diagnosis itself as part of the problem. Winner has accused his field of differentiating itself from prior work in philosophy of technology mostly by ratcheting up complexity: STS parts ways from earlier thinkers like Mumford or Ellul, largely by revealing the complex, dynamic nature of sociotechnical interaction. Research results in STS, Winner argues, particularly in the dominant social shaping tradition, "usually indicate that technological intervention is a multicentered, complex process."[69] In a recent interview in the Spanish design magazine *Diseña*, the historian of technology David Edgerton also criticizes the tendency of STS to make a fetish of complexity: "STS is a complicated way of telling others elementary truths about our world and how it has been made."[70]

I do not fully share these views. But I do want to pause to note that this emphasis on the specificity and dynamism of sociotechnical systems is partly what explains the allure of the so-called Collingridge dilemma mentioned already. Recall that in *The Social Control of Technology*, Collingridge posits that society faces a temporal dilemma in attempting to regulate technology. Try to intervene too soon, and policymakers risk misunderstanding the social impacts of emerging technology and hence do more harm than good. Try to intervene too late, however, and technology will have already become intertwined in the fabric of everyday life. The policymaker then faces a public reliant upon the new affordances and a path dependent techno-social system that will be difficult to redirect.

He may not use the words "interpretive flexibility," but Collingridge's thesis holds that the very complexity of the interplay between the technical and the social means we cannot know in advance what impact the introduction of technology will have on society. And if we cannot know in advance what technology will do or mean, attempts to regulate it are doomed to prematurity. Meanwhile, through the magic of libertarian rhetoric, the Collingridge dilemma becomes the pacing problem—a widely accepted tenet of law and technology that quietly erodes the foundation for regulatory precaution. Complexity of this sort can be paralyzing. There is a tension between getting something right and getting something done.

To address the deficiencies of STS, Latour urges the field to adopt a "stubbornly realist attitude."[71] That phrase describes a lot of legal scholarship

pretty well. As Julie Cohen remarks in the context of surveillance studies, law possesses a certain "relentless pragmatism" in the sense of identifying with, and trying to solve, real-world problems.[72] We come by our pragmatism honestly, by way of American pragmatists like Charles Peirce, John Dewey, and William James, as well as the jurists and reformers they influenced: Oliver Wendall Holmes Jr. (Peirce's friend), Nobel Peace Prize laureate Jane Addams (Dewey's friend), and W. E. B. Du Bois (James's friend and student).[73] "All American lawyers," writes Jack Balkin, "are intellectual descendants of Holmes's pragmatism."[74] While few law and technology scholars stand up and proclaim, "I am a pragmatist!" the vast majority of the literature with which I am familiar attends to problem-solving. Law is a useful science.

Whatever the intellectual history, legal scholarship, in general, and law and technology scholarship, in particular, is replete with specific schemes to safeguard rights and values in light of technological change and calls for reform. Unlike in other disciplines, where to prescribe is to be unscientific, legal scholars expect solutions to come swift on the heels of critique. Like a play in three acts, the paradigmatic law review article or book furnishes context, diagnoses an issue, and then describes what to do about it (*The Future of the Internet*... *And What to Do About It*). There are many law review articles that dispense with the first two acts and simply describe a solution in detail. And of course, being lawyers by training, law professors propose reforms or changes in terms that a court, agency, or legislative body could operationalize, anticipating roadblocks and noting secondary benefits.

In privacy, there have been elegant suggestions to apply strict liability and other aspects of tort, calls to empower federal and state lawmakers, and elaborate suggestions to draw from environmental regulation, equity, copyright, and trade secret.[75] There have been multiple efforts to update and apply 1970s information principles developed by an international body, and multiple efforts to extend fiduciary responsibilities to technology companies.[76] Scholars have looked to confidentiality law, antitrust, technical standards, and "nudges."[77] Scholars have argued for new laws to shore up the structural safeguards to privacy that technology displaces, laws to mandate that the internet forget what it knows, and laws requiring that technology companies give consumers a paid option to use their service without tracking.[78] This is a woefully incomplete list, and it's just privacy law.

The dichotomy I lay out between descriptive STS and prescriptive legal scholarship is not without its problems. Some legal scholars struggle as they move from description to prescription, following up an elaborate doctrinal

analysis with what Deborah Rhode calls "touchingly naïve strategies for change."[79] And I am, of course, well aware that legal scholarship's normativity is under assault from the inside—by Pierre Schlag, Paul Kahn, and Stanley Fish of "save the world on your own time" fame, among others.[80] Critics decry normative legal scholarship as empty and misleading, or little more than a heavily footnoted legal brief filed on one's own behalf. (Though, as West and Citron point out, scholarship can and does lead to legal change.) To me, it seems self-evident that discussions of law are discussions of justice. But that view is not everywhere held.

Law and STS

Technology's relationship to people and society is easy to misunderstand. Law professors can and should draw from STS to get a better handle on this unique, mercurial social fact. It is neither sufficient nor desirable, however, for law and technology simply to import STS wholesale into the legal analysis of artifacts and technical systems. Such a strategy risks abandoning important aspects of American legal scholarship, generally, and law and technology, in particular, including the normativity and pragmatism that permeates the academy. How, then, should law and technology deploy STS?

I do not mean to suggest the field of law and technology is wholly ignorant of STS.[81] Some work invokes STS almost defensively, that is, to reassure the reader that the author understands the relationship between technology and society is complex. This is true to an extent of Tribe—who, again, did not have the benefit of many of the works I have cited. Yochai Benkler's *The Wealth of Networks*, while formally a political economy analysis of information policy, commits to STS-like nuance in its treatment of the role of technology in human affairs.[82] More specifically, Benkler rejects the "naïve determinism" of Mumford and Marshall McLuhan in favor of an understanding of technology as setting "some parameters of individual and social action."[83] Benkler's book remains largely true to this commitment, but the references to Winner end at the introduction.

Other scholars deploy STS, and especially social shaping of technology theory, to critique the law. In a 2018 article, STS scholar Meg Leta Jones tests the theory of "technological exceptionalism" in law against a variety of contexts, including photography, computing, and robotics. She finds that law and technology scholars routinely overlook cultural shifts from sources other

than technology.[84] Internet governance scholar Viktor Mayer-Schönberger invokes Latour in critiquing Lessig for missing the "mutuality of influences between technology and society."[85] Without citing STS as such, Balkin makes a similar move in critiquing my work on robotics law, noting that "the path of robotics law" cannot be predicted in advance, but will emerge from the interplay between the technology and the "regulatory scene."[86] Cohen invokes STS to critique the concept of regulation by code as simplistic, preferring an account that understands law as helping to "infus[e] regulation into the artifacts and practices of daily life."[87]

Law and technology scholars have leveraged the concepts and methods of STS to investigate technology more thoroughly. The idea that artifacts have politics was at the heart of communications-trained privacy law scholar Woodrow Hartzog's important book *Privacy's Blueprint*.[88] Design is a series of decisions that affects individual and group behavior and the distribution of power itself, and hence must be a focal point of privacy law and policy. In addition to her critique of deterministic legal scholarship, Jones leverages history and case study to unpack techno-social phenomenon, from the right to be forgotten online, to the life and death of the internet cookie.[89] Legally trained STS scholar Karen Levy brought the field's methodological toolkit usefully to bear in a variety of contexts, from agricultural technology to transportation.[90] Dan Burk leveraged STS in his work on the social construction of patents.[91]

In *Configuring the Network Self*, Cohen develops a "hybrid" approach to information policy that integrates lessons of STS, the capabilities approach from institutional economics, and a roughly "postmodern" conception of the self to revisit and re-characterize the central questions of the field.[92] These interdisciplinary moves position Cohen to break new ground. A working knowledge of STS enables Cohen to better trace the complex distributions of policy and power across people, networks, and things. Embracing the capabilities approach—especially an extension of Martha Nussbaum's enumerated capability of "play"—enables Cohen to articulate a defensible normative aim for law and technology. Cohen draws from postmodernism to better resist liberal political theory's oversimplified conception of the individual as stable, autonomous, and disembodied (i.e., not situated).

Mireille Hildebrandt's approach in *Smart Technology and the End(s) of Law* draws from STS, including the role of narrative, to diagnose a problem with society and a concomitant deficiency in the rule of law as presently configured.[93] While she does not go as far as Brett Frischmann and Evan

Selinger in *Re-Engineering Humanity*[94]—or Ellul and Heidegger for that matter, whom she dismissed as deterministically dystopian—Hildebrandt is clearly concerned with the ways digital technology has come to mediate human behavior and undermine agency.[95] The law, based on the affordances of the printing press, is not fighting fire with fire when it comes to the collapse of the digital and physical into the "onlife." Her solution involves updating the affordances of law itself by embedding the rule of law directly into artifacts and systems.

As interpretive flexibility would predict, STS scholars do not always reach the same conclusions. Writing with Kenneth Bamberger, Deirdre Mulligan explores the social and economic forces driving privacy compliance in the United States "on the ground."[96] Their interviews with privacy professionals appeared to depict a deeper commitment to privacy than our patchwork legal system requires. Legal sociologist Ari Ezra Waldman, meanwhile, blends qualitative sociology and legal analysis to tell a different story: Privacy professionals in the technology sector subverted privacy interests, turning legal commitments into hollow compliance rituals.[97]

The best way to incorporate STS into legal analysis, to me, is to build its core insights into careful method. Hence, the promise of this book: a methodical approach. Chapter Three lays out a step-by-step approach for the legal analysis of technology. The aim of the approach is to add structure and rigor to law and technology in ways that overcome technological incapacity without fundamentally reconstituting the field. The first two steps in particular—definition and envisioning—borrow heavily from STS. These steps require the law and technology scholar to carefully define the technology under examination, attend to its contingency, and explore its potential to influence individual and group behavior.

Ultimately what STS can do for law and technology scholarship is to help us layer in a more nuanced understanding of our subject matter so that we can resist over-simplification and error. The last two steps of the approach tend to repay the favor. Step three requires a careful statement of the normative baseline against which analysis and prescription will occur. This step asks: is the project aimed at preserving the status quo ex ante in light of technological disruption? Or does the project view the technology under examination as an invitation to inventory values and pursue a more just course in light of novel affordances? Step four constitutes a thorough examination of the levers of power. It asks: what are the specific means available to restore the law's expectations in light of technological change, channel the

technology in the public interest, or otherwise promote human flourishing? And are there tradeoffs of these different approaches?

My own contact with STS has led me to see technology as a contingent bundle of affordances, rather than a stable construct, and to foreground the social and cultural forces behind it. This informs how I approach a law and technology project. I now see artificial intelligence, for example, as a set of techniques whose primary affordance—pattern recognition—reinforces Western predilections for categorization while breaking down legal categories such as intent and privacy.

I have also had occasion to step back and look at STS holistically. A challenge common to STS and to law is capturing the nuance of interpretive flexibility while still acknowledging technology's "politics." On the one hand, technology is contingent and nondeterministic, beholden to social forces in both its development and societal trajectory. On the other hand, technology does carry certain "politics" and "affordances." While code is not always law, the design of everyday things matters to social experience.

Legal analysis must acknowledge and attend to this tension directly. We should be wary of accepting particular instantiations of technology as inevitable or evolutionary, and humble in our predictions as to the path the technology is likely to take. The alternative is invariable error. At the same time, we must acknowledge that the characteristics of various technologies as deployed—from the train to the internet to robotics and Artificial Intelligence—shape human behavior, and hence the range of appropriate legal responses. The alternative is policy paralysis.

The challenge for law and technology, then, is considerable. Legal scholars, policymakers, and other jurists must avoid the common pitfalls that underpin technological incapacity while simultaneously setting guardrails for an uncertain future. In my view, this necessitates a methodical approach.

Notes

1. THE SOCIAL DILEMMA (Exposure Labs 2020).
2. *See* LANGDON WINNER, THE WHALE AND THE REACTOR (University of Chicago Press 2020) (reprinted).
3. *Compare* LAWRENCE LESSIG, CODE AND OTHER LAWS OF CYBERSPACE (Basic Books 1999), *and* Joel R. Reidenberg, *Lex Informatica: The Formulation of Information Policy Rules through Technology*, 76 TEX. L. REV. 553 (1997), *with* Langdon Winner, *Do Artifacts Have Politics?* 109 DAEDALUS 121 (1980), *and* Bruno Latour, *Where Are the Missing Masses? The Sociology of a Few Mundane Artifacts*, *in* SHAPING TECH. / BLDG. SOC'Y: STUD. IN SOCIOTECHNICAL CHANGE 152 (Wiebe Bijker & John Law eds., MIT Press 1992).

4. *Compare* Jonathan L. Zittrain, *The Generative Internet*, 119 Harvard L. Rev. 1974 (2006), *with* Ivan Illich, Tools for Conviviality (Marion Boyars 1990) (reprinted).
5. Max Weber, Politics as a Vocation (Duncker & Humblot 2010) (1919).
6. Ronald Dworkin, Law's Empire (Belknap Press 1986); Robert M. Cover, *Violence and the Word*, 95 Yale L.J. 1601 (1986); Robin West, Normative Jurisprudence: An Introduction (Cambridge University Press 2011).
7. Julie E. Cohen, Configuring the Network Self: Law, Code, and the Play of Everyday (Yale University Press 2012).
8. Thomas S. Kuhn, The Structure of Scientific Revolutions (University of Chicago Press 2d ed. 1970).
9. John Law, *STS as Method*, *in* The Handbook of Science and Technology Studies 32 (Edward J. Hackett et al. eds., MIT Press 4th ed. 2016).
10. Robert McGinn, Science, Technology, and Society (Prentice Hall 1991); Sheila Jasanoff, *A Field of Its Own: The Emergence of Science and Technology Studies*, *in* The Oxford Handbook of Interdisciplinarity (Robert Frodeman ed., Oxford University Press 2d ed. 2017); Peter Dear & Sheila Jasanoff, *Dismantling Boundaries in Science and Technology Studies*, 1010 Isis 759 (2020).
11. Bruno Latour & Steve Woolgar, Laboratory Life (Princeton University Press 1979).
12. Michel Callon, *Some Elements of a Sociology of Translation: Domestication of the Scallops and the Fisherman of St. Brieuc Bay*, 32 Soc. Rev. 196 (1984).
13. Sheila Jasanoff & Sang-Hyun Kim, *Containing the Atom: Sociotechnical Imaginaries and Nuclear Power in the United States and South Korea*, 47 Minerva 119 (2009). *See also* Sheila Jasanoff & Sang-Hyun Kim, Dreamscapes of Modernity: Sociotechnical Imaginaries and the Fabrication of Power (University of Chicago Press 2015).
14. Sheila Jasanoff, *A Field of Its Own: The Emergence of Science and Technology Studies*, *in* The Oxford Handbook of Interdisciplinarity 173 (Robert Frodeman ed., Oxford University Press 2d ed. 2017).
15. Sally Wyatt, *Technological Determinism Is Dead; Long Live Technological Determinism*, *in* The handbook of science and technology studies (Edward J. Hackett et al. eds., MIT Press 3rd ed. 2008).
16. Thomas P. Hughes, *Technological Momentum in History: Hydrogenation in Germany 1898-1933*, 44 Past and Present 106 (1969).
17. Ivan Illich, Tools for Conviviality (Marion Boyars 1990) (reprinted).
18. Judy Wajcman, *Feminist Theories of Technology*, 34 Cambridge J. Econ. 143, 144 (2010).
19. Mar Hicks, Programmed Inequality: How Britain Discarded Women Technologists and Lost Its Edge in Computing (MIT Press 2018).
20. Ruth Schwartz Cohen, More Work for Mother: The Ironies of Household Technology from the Open Hearth to the Microwave (Basic Books 1983).
21. Donna Haraway, *Manifesto for Cyborgs: Science, Technology, and Socialist Feminism in the 1980s*, 1985 Socialist Rev. 65 (1985).
22. Simone Browne, Dark Matters: On the Surveillance of Blackness (Duke University Press 2015).
23. Safiya Umoja Noble, *Missed Connections: What Search Engines Say About Women*, Bitch Magazine (Spring 2012).
24. Ruha Benjamin, Race After Technology: Abolitionist Tools for the New Jim Code (Polity Press 2019).
25. Lisa Nakamura, Digitizing Race: Visual Cultures of the Internet (University of Minnesota Press 2007).
26. Alondra Nelson, Thuy Linh N. Tu, & Alicia Headlam Hines, Technicolor: race, technology, and everyday life 3 (New York University Press 2001).
27. Charlton McIlwain, Black Software: The Internet and Racial Justice, from the AfroNet to Black Lives Matter (Oxford University Press 2019).
28. André Brock, Jr., Distributed Blackness (New York University Press 2020).
29. Alondra Nelson, Thuy Linh N. Tu, & Alicia Headlam Hines, Technicolor: race, technology, and everyday life 3 (New York University Press 2001).
30. Judy Wajcman, *Feminist Theories of Technology*, 34 Cambridge J. Econ. 143, 147 (2010).
31. Simone Browne, Dark Matters: On the Surveillance of Blackness (Duke University Press 2015).

32. Toby Beauchamp, Going Stealth: Transgender Politics and U.S. Surveillance Practices (Duke University Press 2019).
33. Safiya Umoja Noble, Algorithms of Oppression: How Search Engines Reinforce Racism (New York University Press 2018).
34. Lyria Bennett Moses, *Agents of Change: How the Law "Copes" with Technological Change*, 20 Griffith L. Rev. 763 (2011).
35. Julie E. Cohen, *Cyberspace As/And Space*, 107 Colum. L. Rev. 210 (2007).
36. Bruno Latour, *Technology Is Society Made Durable*, 38 Soc. Rev. 103, 105 (1990).
37. Bruno Latour, *Technology Is Society Made Durable*, 38 Soc. Rev. 103, 105 (1990); Oliver Wendell Holmes, Jr., *The Path of the Law*, 10 Harv. L. Rev. 457 (1897).
38. Ivan Illich, Tools for Conviviality (Marion Boyars 1990) (reprinted).
39. Tim Wu, *When Code Isn't Law*, 89 Va. L. Rev. 679 (2003).
40. Jack Goldsmith & Tim Wu, Who Controls the Internet?: Illusions of a Borderless World (Oxford University Press 2006).
41. James Grimmelmann, *Regulation by Software*, 114 Yale L. J. 1719 (2005).
42. Jack Balkin, *The Path of Robotics Law*, 6 Calif. L. Rev. Cir. 45, 47 (2015), responding to Ryan Calo, *Robotics and the Lessons of Cyberlaw*, 103 Calif. L. Rev. 513 (2015).
43. A. Michael Froomkin, *The Metaphor Is the Key: Cryptography, the Clipper Chip, and the Constitution*, 143 U. Pa. L. Rev. 709 (1995).
44. Daniel J. Solove, *Privacy and Power: Computer Databases and Metaphors for Information Privacy*, 53 Stan. L. Rev. 1393 (2001).
45. Sheila Jasanoff & Sang-Hyun Kim, *Containing the Atom: Sociotechnical Imaginaries and Nuclear Power in the United States and South Korea*, 47 Minerva 119 (June 2009). *See also* Sheila Jasanoff & Sang-Hyun Kim, Dreamscapes of Modernity: Sociotechnical Imaginaries and the Fabrication of Power (University of Chicago Press 2015).
46. *See* Sally Wyatt, *Technological Determinism is Dead; Long Live Technological Determinism*, *in* The Handbook of Science and Technology Studies (Edward J. Hackett et al. eds., MIT Press 3rd ed. 2008); Merritt Roe Smith & Leo Marx, Does Technology Drive History?: The Dilemma of Technological Determinism (MIT Press 1994).
47. Bryan Pfaffenberger, *Technological Dramas*, 17 Sci., Tech., & Hum. Values 282 (1992).
48. Ben Williams, *Black Secret Technology: Detroit Techno and The Information Age*, *in* Technicolor: Race, Technology, and Everyday Life (Alondra Nelson et al. eds., New York University Press 2001).
49. Donna Haraway, *Teddy Bear Patriarchy: Taxidermy in the Garden of Eden, New York City, 1908-1936*, *in* Grasping the World (1st ed., Routledge 2004) 20.
50. Orin S. Kerr, *An Equilibrium-Adjustment Theory of the Fourth Amendment*, 125 Harv. L. Rev. 476 (2011).
51. *See* Mireille Hildebrandt, Smart Technologies and the End(s) of Law (Edward Elgar 2015); Joshua Fairfield, Runaway Technology: Can Law Keep Up? (Cambridge University Press 2021).
52. The reference is to the famous debate between HLA Hart and Lon Fuller about easy and hard cases. *See* H. L. A. Hart, *Positivism and the Separation of Law and Morals*, 71 Harv. L. Rev. 593 (1958); Lon L. Fuller, *Positivism and Fidelity to Law — A Reply to Professor Hart*, 71 Harv. L. Rev. 630 (1958).
53. Bruno Latour, The Making of Law: An Ethnography of the Conseil d'État (Polity 2010).
54. Lawrence Lessig, Code and Other Laws of Cyberspace (Basic Books 1999). *See also* Lawrence Lessig, *The Law of the Horse: What Cyberlaw Might Teach*, 113 Harv. L. Rev. 501 (1999).
55. Richard Delgado, *Norms and Normal Science: Toward a Critique of Normativity in Legal Thought*, 139 U. Pa. L. Rev. 933 (1991).
56. Robert M. Cover, *Violence and the Word*, 95 Yale L. J. 1601 (1986).
57. I associate this idea with the earlier work of Lon Fuller, especially *The Law in Quest of Itself*, which is based on three lectures Fuller gave in the late 1930s. But Dworkin is, and should be, credited for developing a full-throated account of the relationship between what the law is and what it should be. See Ronald M. Dworkin, *Integrity in Law*, *in* Law's Empire (Belknap Press 1986); Lon L. Fuller, The Law in Quest of Itself (Lawbook Exchange 1966).
58. Ronald M. Dworkin, *Integrity in Law*, *in* Law's Empire (Belknap Press 1986); Robert M. Cover, *Violence and the Word*, 95 Yale L. J. 1601 (1986).

59. Richard A. Posner, *The Problematics of Moral and Legal Theory*, 111 HARV. L. REV. 1637 (1997).
60. Martha Nussbaum, *Still Worthy of Praise*, 111 HARV. L. REV. 1776 (1998).
61. *See* Robin West, *The Ethics of Normative Legal Scholarship*, 101 MARQ. L. REV. 981 (2018); Robin West, *The Contested Value of Normative Legal Scholarship*, 66 J. LEGAL EDUC. 6 (2016); ROBIN WEST, NORMATIVE JURISPRUDENCE: AN INTRODUCTION (2011); Danielle K. Citron & Robin West, *On Legal Scholarship*, *in* CURRENT ISSUES IN LEGAL EDUCATION (2014).
62. Robin West, *The Contested Value of Normative Legal Scholarship*, 66 J. LEGAL EDUC. 6, 7 (2016).
63. Danielle K. Citron & Robin West, *On Legal Scholarship*, *in* CURRENT ISSUES IN LEGAL EDUCATION (2014). See generally Ronald M. Dworkin, *Integrity in Law*, *in* LAW'S EMPIRE (Belknap Press 1986).
64. JONATHAN ZITTRAIN, THE FUTURE OF THE INTERNET—AND HOW TO STOP IT 225 (Yale University Press 2008).
65. Langdon Winner, *Upon Opening the Black Box and Finding it Empty: Social Constructivism and the Philosophy of Technology*, 18 SCI., TECH., & HUM. VALUES 362 (1992).
66. *Id.*
67. Bruno Latour, *Why has Critique Run out of Steam? From Matters of Fact to Matters of Concern*, 30 CRIT. INQ. 225 (2004).
68. ROBIN WEST, NORMATIVE JURISPRUDENCE: AN INTRODUCTION 7 (2011).
69. Langdon Winner, *Upon Opening the Black Box and Finding it Empty: Social Constructivism and the Philosophy of Technology*, 18 SCI., TECH., & HUM. VALUES 362 (1992).
70. David Egerton, Hugo Palmarola, & Pedro Álvarez Caselli, *Some Problems with the Concept of "Technology" in Design: Interview with David Edgerton (Interview.2)*, 18 DISEÑA 1 (2021).
71. Bruno Latour, *Why Has Critique Run Out of Steam? From Matters of Fact to Matters of Concern*, 30 CRIT. INQ. 225 (2004).
72. JULIE E. COHEN, CONFIGURING THE NETWORK SELF: LAW, CODE, AND THE PLAY OF EVERYDAY (Yale University Press 2012).
73. These were members of the Metaphysical Club. *See* Oliver Wendell Holmes, Jr., *The Path of the Law*, 10 HARV. L. REV. 457 (1897); JANE ADDAMS, TWENTY YEARS AT HULL HOUSE: WITH AUTOBIOGRAPHICAL NOTES (University of Illinois Press 1990); W. E. B. DU BOIS, DARK PRINCESS: A ROMANCE (Oxford University Press 2007).
74. Jack Balkin, *The Path of Robotics Law*, 6 CALIF. L. REV. CIR. 45 (2015).
75. *See, e.g.*, Danielle K. Citron, *Reservoirs of Danger: The Evolution of Public and Privacy Law at the Dawn of the Information Age*, 80 S. CAL. L. REV. 241 (2007); Andrew J. McClurg, *A Thousand Words Are Worth a Picture: A Privacy Tort Response to Consumer Data Profiling*, 98 NW. U. L. REV. 63 (2003) (proposing the appropriation tort as a remedy against data profiling); Jessica Litman, *Information Privacy/Information Property*, 52 STAN. L. REV. 1283 (2000) (suggesting that tort law might support a workable approach to data privacy); Andrew Jay McClurg, *Bringing Privacy Law Out of the Closet: A Tort Theory of Liability for Intrusions in Public Places*, 73 N.C. L. REV. 989 (1995) (arguing that the right to privacy in tort law must be expanded to cover invasions of privacy in a "public" place); Robert Gellman, *A Better Way to Approach Privacy Policy in the United States: Establish a Non-Regulatory Privacy Protection Board*, 54 HASTINGS L.J. 1183 (2003) (claiming that the United States needs a federal privacy agency); Dennis D. Hirsch, *Protecting the Inner Environment: What Privacy Regulation Can Learn From Environmental Law*, 41 GEO. L. REV. 1 (2006) (posing that environmental law can serve as a useful model for information privacy); Pauline T. Kim, *Data-Driven Discrimination At Work*, 58 WM. & MARY L. REV. 857 (2000) (proposing to rethink antidiscrimination doctrine to address biased outcomes produced by decision-making algorithms); Julie Cohen, *Examined Lives: Informational Privacy and the Subject as Object*, 52 STAN. L. REV. 1373–1438 (2000) (arguing that similar to copyright law, a theory of informational privacy should be crafted to preserve the benefits of sunlight); Sharon K. Sandeen, *Relative Privacy: What Privacy Advocates Can Learn from Trade Secret Law*, 2006 MICH. ST. L. REV. 667 (2006) (inviting privacy law to follow the path of trade secret law).
76. *See* Jack Balkin, *The Fiduciary Model of Privacy*, 134 HARV. L. REV. F. 11, 16 n.25 (2020) (listing examples). The earliest North American scholar to introduce a fiduciary model for information privacy was Ian Kerr. Later scholars include Dan Solove, Ari Waldman, Neil Richards, and Woodrow Hartzog, to name a few. *Id.*
77. *See, e.g.*, Woodrow Hartzog, *Reviving Implied Confidentiality*, 89 IND. L. J. 763 (2014) (proposing the revival of implied confidentiality to resolve the problems caused by the disclosure of personal information on the internet); Daniel J. Solove & Neil Richards, *Privacy's Other Path: Recovering*

the Law of Confidentiality, 96 GEO. L.J. 123 (2007) (arguing that American privacy law should learn from the English law of confidence, which recognizes and enforces expectations of trust within relationships); G. Michael Harvey, *Confidentiality: A Measured Response to the Failure of Privacy*, 140 U. PA. L. REV. 2385 (1992) (advocating for the replacement of the private-facts tort with a new tort based on breach of confidence); Frank Pasquale, *Privacy, Antitrust, and Power*, 20 GEO. MASON L. REV. 1009 (2013); Erika M. Douglas, *The New Antitrust/Data Privacy Law Interface*, 2021 YALE L. J. F. 647 (2021).

78. *E.g.*, Harry Surden, *Structural Rights in Privacy*, 60 SMU L. REV. 1605 (2007); Ryan Calo, *Digital Market Manipulation*, 82 GEO. WASH. L. REV. 995 (2014).
79. Deborah L Rhode, *Legal Scholarship*, 115 HARV. L. REV. 1327, 1342 (2002).
80. *See* Pierre Schlag, *Normativity and the Politics of Form*, 139 U. PA. L. REV. 801 (1991); PAUL W KAHN, THE CULTURAL STUDY OF LAW: RECONSTRUCTING LEGAL SCHOLARSHIP (University of Chicago Press 1999); STANLEY FISH, SAVE THE WORLD ON YOUR OWN TIME (Oxford University Press 2012).
81. As this is a book about law and technology, I have focused on the "T" in STS, and not the "S" for science. The work of STS scholars like Jasanoff, and legal scholars like Jennifer Mnookin, have had concrete impacts on, e.g., the credibility of forensic science and the admissibility of scientific expertise at trial. *See, e.g.*, Jennifer Mnookin, *The Uncertain Future of Forensic Science*, 147 DAEDALUS 99 (Fall 2018); Jennifer Mnookin, *Constructing Evidence and Educating Juries: The Case for Modular, Made-In-Advance Expert Evidence about Eyewitness Identifications and False Confessions*, 93 TEX. L. REV. 1811 (2015); Jennifer Mnookin & David H. Kaye, *Confronting Science: Expert Evidence and the Confrontation Clause*, 2012 SUP. CT. REV. 99 (2013).
82. YOCHAI BENKLER, THE WEALTH OF NETWORKS: HOW SOCIAL PRODUCTION TRANSFORMS MARKETS AND FREEDOM (Yale University Press 2006).
83. *Id.*
84. Meg Leta Jones, *Does Technology Drive Law? The Dilemma of Technological Exceptionalism in Cyberlaw*, 2018 J.L. TECH & POL'Y 249 (2018).
85. Viktor Mayer-Schönberger, *Demystifying Lessig*, 2008 WIS. L. REV. 713, 740 (2008).
86. Jack Balkin, *The Path of Robotics Law*, 6 CALIF. L. REV. CIR. 45, 50 (2015), responding to Ryan Calo, *Robotics and the Lessons of Cyberlaw*, 103 CALIF. L. REV. 513 (2015). See also Margot E. Kaminski, *Technological "Disruption" of the Law's Imagined Scene: Some Lessons from* Lex Informatica, 36 BERKELEY TECH. L.J. 883, n.69 (2021) (discussing the relationship between "imagined regulatory scene" and "sociotechnical imaginaries").
87. Julie E. Cohen, *Pervasively Distributed Copyright Enforcement*, 95 GEO. L.J. 1, 21 (2006).
88. WOODROW HARTZOG, PRIVACY'S BLUEPRINT: THE BATTLE TO CONTROL THE DESIGN OF NEW TECHNOLOGIES (Harvard University Press 2018).
89. *See, e.g.*, MEG LETA JONES, CTRL + Z: THE RIGHT TO BE FORGOTTEN (New York University Press 2016); Meg Leta Jones, *Cookies: A Legacy of Controversy*, 4 INTERNET HISTORIES, Special Issue on Legacy Systems 87 (2020); MEG LETA JONES, THE CHARACTER OF CONSENT: THE HISTORY OF COOKIES AND FUTURE OF TECHNOLOGY POLICY (MIT Press 2024).
90. *See, e.g.*, Karen E. C. Levy, *The Contexts of Control: Information, Power, and Truck-Driving Work*, 31 INFO. SOC. 160 (2015); Solon Barocas, Karen Levy, & Alexandra Mateescu, *Reap What You Sow? Automation, Information, and Economic Distribution on the Farm*, Paper presented at We Robot Conference 2019. Available at: https://robots.law.miami.edu/2019/wp-content/uploads/2019/03/BarocasLevyMateescu_WeRobot.pdf
91. *E.g.*, Dan L. Burk, *Patents in Action*, 63 JURIMETRICS J. 221 (2023).
92. JULIE E. COHEN, CONFIGURING THE NETWORK SELF: LAW, CODE, AND THE PLAY OF EVERYDAY (Yale University Press 2012).
93. MIREILLE HILDEBRANDT, SMART TECHNOLOGY AND THE END(S) OF LAW: NOVEL ENTANGLEMENTS OF LAW AND TECHNOLOGY (Edward Elgar 2015).
94. BRETT FRISCHMANN & EVAN SELINGER, RE-ENGINEERING HUMANITY (Cambridge University Press 2018).
95. MIREILLE HILDEBRANDT, SMART TECHNOLOGY AND THE END(S) OF LAW: NOVEL ENTANGLEMENTS OF LAW AND TECHNOLOGY (Edward Elgar 2015).
96. KENNETH A. BAMBERGER & DEIRDRE K. MULLIGAN, PRIVACY ON THE GROUND: DRIVING CORPORATE BEHAVIOR IN THE UNITED STATES AND EUROPE (MIT Press 2015).
97. ARI EZRA WALDMAN, INDUSTRY UNBOUND: THE INSIDE STORY OF PRIVACY, DATA, AND CORPORATE POWER (Cambridge University Press 2021).

Suggested Readings

Julie Cohen, *Studying Law Studying Surveillance*, 13 (1) SURVEILLANCE & SOC. 91–101 (Jan. 2015).

Sheila Jasanoff, *A Field of Its Own: The Emergence of Science and Technology Studies*, *in* THE OXFORD HANDBOOK OF INTERDISCIPLINARITY 173 (Robert Frodeman ed., 2d ed. 2017).

Bruno Latour, *Why has Critique Run out of Steam? From Matters of Fact to Matters of Concern*, 30 CRIT. INQ. 225 (2004).

ROBIN WEST & DANIELLE KEATS CITRON, *On Legal Scholarship*, *in* CURRENT ISSUES IN L. EDU. (2014).

Langdon Winner, *Upon Opening the Black Box and Finding it Empty: Social Constructivism and the Philosophy of Technology*, 18 SCI., TECH., & HUM. VALUES 362 (1992).

THREE
THOUGH THIS BE MADNESS

Introduction

"For to be possessed of a vigorous mind is not enough," writes René Descartes in his seventeenth century treatise, *Discourse on Methods*. "The prime requisite is rightly to apply it."[1] Descartes claimed no monopoly on how rightly to apply a vigorous mind. But his intuitions that analysis should proceed from formal methods have had a profound and lasting influence on scholarly discourse.

The legal academy is replete with vigorous minds. Yet, law professors expend relatively little effort on the development or application of formal methods. Adjacent work in the social sciences or the humanities devotes significant attention to methodology. Papers in these and many other fields have methods sections; law review articles almost never do. As Deborah Rhode observes, the "vast majority of legal scholars" engage primarily in "doctrinal analysis," an approach that "requires no special expertise beyond what is available through traditional law school training."[2] Former Harvard Law Dean Martha Minow's oft-cited field guide to "archetypal legal scholarship" makes only glancing reference to formal methods in mapping the intellectual terrain.[3]

The legal academy nevertheless places a quiet premium on method. More and more legal scholars hold a PhD in another discipline, where method is paramount. The corners of the legal academy that have embraced methodology to any significant degree—law and economics, critical theory, and empirical legal studies, to name a few—tend to have a disproportionate impact on the shape of legal discourse. There is an advantage simply from inviting a consistent approach to legal or societal problems, even if the approach is simplistic, and even if the scholar possesses no formal training in the methods themselves. A law and economics scholar knows to analyze doctrine by reference to incentives and welfare maximization. They are off to the races, while law and technology scholars are still contemplating the horse.

Law and Technology. Ryan Calo, Oxford University Press. © Ryan Calo 2025.
DOI: 10.1093/9780197526170.003.0004

Methods have many benefits, from surfacing assumptions to encouraging care and rigor. Methods are arguably what distinguish scholarship from other modes of inquiry—which is why an inattention to methodology would be unthinkable in many disciplines. Methods constitute an additional check on the reliability of scholarly evidence and conclusions, beyond verifying that someone else made a similar claim in a previous source. Methods are also themselves subject to analysis and refinement. Every application of a method represents a chance to critique and improve that method, such that future investigation benefits from past.

The entire legal academy would likely benefit from greater attention to method. But the law and technology field is especially situated to gain from a clear methodology. As discussed in detail in Chapter One, the social fact of technology possesses qualities that tend to confuse and mislead the legal observer. Technology poses as inevitable when it is nearly always contingent; technology hides human will and makes a shell game of responsibility; technology invites regulatory paralysis, while placing values and rights into a posture of constant defense. Individually and together, these facets of technology present an exceptional challenge to law and governance to which a successful analysis must attend. Given technology's tendency toward mystification, a clear, step-by-step approach represents our best chance to overcome this technological fog and produce knowledge on par with sister fields.

A *shared* methodology holds a further advantage. A central aim of this book is to develop a formal approach to law and technology capable of navigating the ways in which technology daunts and confuses, leading to specific consequences for law and legal institutions. Yet, avoiding pitfalls is but one advantage. I'm increasingly of the view that the principal reason law and technology has yet to cohere as a field is the lack of a rigorous and *consistent* approach. A methodology that resonates with and encompasses what law and technology scholars already tend to do also holds the potential to unify the field beyond a common subject matter.

Over the years, many scholars have offered thoughts on law and technology in theory. There are, indeed, entire symposia devoted to the nature of law and technology dating back decades. These interesting and fruitful efforts aim primarily to distinguish the analysis of technology from other forms of legal inquiry, or otherwise explicate the conceptual interplay between law and things. Their aim is to develop "general," "coherent," or "synthetic" accounts of the field.[4] I have read and engaged these authors; their work deeply

informs my perspective. But their aim is not to articulate a method. The goal of law and technology theory is not, as Arthur Cockfield and Jason Pridmore put it, to "replace the traditional technology law avenues of inquiry into technology law, assuming such a move would be feasible."[5]

In their 2021 article *Structuring TechLaw*, Rebecca Crootof and BJ Ard develop a tripartite framework "designed to encourage a more thoughtful resolution of structural techlaw questions." Their framework—which they refer to alternately as a "methodological structure"—encourages law and technology scholars to draw three distinctions: between types of legal uncertainty, between permissive and precautionary approaches, and between extant law, new law, and wholesale reassessment to address legal uncertainty. These three distinctions shed much light on law and technology as a field, but they do not amount to a method by which to analyze the legal aspects of specific technologies.[6]

There are, of course, limits to methodology. "Each method should be regarded as offering potential opportunities not available by other means," writes psychologist Joseph McGrath, "but also as having inherent limitations."[7] Adherence to a common methodology can unify an otherwise disparate field. It can promote rigor and accountability. But, there are other ways of promoting these values, and perhaps dangers to overemphasizing a single approach. Descartes's caveat is well-taken: "My present design, then, is not to teach the method which each ought to follow . . . but solely to describe the way in which I have endeavored to conduct my own."

New or veteran, I invite revision and critique. A methodical approach to law and technology offers the opportunity to advance our substantive understanding of specific legal questions about artifacts and technical systems, while simultaneously improving the tools that we have to promote that understanding overall. Each application of a methodology, after all, is an opportunity to refine it. I envision the process of embracing methodology within law and technology to be a garden of forking paths, with (hopefully) many gardeners.

The methodical approach that I detail below seeks to parallel what most law and technology scholars are already doing. We share a set of intellectual tools—defining, analogizing, distinguishing—consistent with common law training. As alluded to in the Introduction, law and technology scholars also adopt more particular, if tacit and inconsistent, methods. The primary framework is the *disruption approach*, introduced via cyberlaw through Lawrence Lessig's concept of "latent ambiguities."[8] Most law and technology

scholarship focuses on how the introduction of a given technology has disrupted or changed our respective rights and responsibilities, and offers prescriptions for how to restore the legal status quo ex ante.

The secondary method—what Lyria Bennett Moses calls "the road not taken" in law and technology scholarship—is *technology assessment*.[9] Technology or "tech" assessment is a holistic approach to planning for the introduction of new technology into society—an activity Laurence Tribe referred to as "channeling technology through law." Tech assessment is largely forward-looking and relies heavily on cost-benefit analysis as its chief mode of analysis. The goal of tech assessment is to help governments and communities maximize the benefits of emerging technology while minimizing the harms.

Law and technology scholars overwhelmingly use disruption or tech assessment. We make other moves too. But a methodical approach to law and technology that overlooks either disruption or assessment will be rejected out of hand.

A final word on terminology: some social scientists draw a distinction between three concepts related to research—paradigm, methodology, and method. The first term, associated with Thomas Kuhn, of "paradigm shift" fame,[10] refers to the overarching criteria for knowledge and validity. What is the researcher trying to learn and how do they know when they have succeeded in learning it? Examples of paradigms include constructivist, positivist, or critical. Most legal scholars within and beyond law and technology tend to be pragmatists, along the lines of Oliver Wendell Holmes Jr., in the sense that they aspire to solve real-world problems using whatever means turn out to be useful.

Many scholars use the second and third terms—methodology and method—interchangeably, as I have done thus far in this chapter. But some draw a further distinction. A *methodology* represents the overall approach to research, including the intellectual or epistemic framework, within which investigation occurs; a *method* refers to a specific process or tool by which to tackle a given research problem.[11] In many ways, a methodology is best understood as a common set of intellectual commitments and assumptions. A method is the actual process the researcher follows—be it qualitative, quantitative, archival, analytic, or "mixed"—in understanding and addressing the problems under review.

Chapter Two laid out many of the methodological commitments and assumptions of law and technology, including assumptions about the nature

of the object under investigation and the field's normative and pragmatic orientation. Now, I turn to the step-by-step process of applying legal analysis to technical artifacts and systems. Specifically, in this chapter, I lay out a process that formalizes the tacit methods of law and technology scholarship by surfacing the author's intent and assumptions and encouraging rigor at each step of analysis. The intention is to be specific enough to improve legal analysis of technology while preserving the contours of what most law and technology scholars already do.[12]

Some of the steps invite law and technology scholars to draw from the methods and knowledge base of other disciplines, such as STS, value sensitive design, and affordance theory. To paraphrase the original *Legend of Zelda*, it can be dangerous to go alone. The law and technology scholar has a range of paths to formulating an accurate mental model of the technology under observation, from formal partnership with technologists to running thoughts and work product by trusted colleagues in other departments. A methodical approach to law and technology can and should reach across disciplines when warranted, just as empirical legal studies, law and literature, and law and economics can and should draw from social science, literary theory, and economic methods, respectively.

It is precisely to avoid becoming mired in such distinctions, however, that I refer to the process on offer as a "methodical approach" to law and technology, rather than a law and technology method or methodology per se. The underlying goal is to realize the benefits of method—surfacing assumptions, avoiding confusion, attending to positionality, providing tools of investigation, introducing rigor and iterative improvement—while preserving the normativity, pragmatism, and other characteristics of contemporary law and technology scholarship.

I also want to be clear to distinguish between *research* and *write up*. The methodical approach asks the law and technology scholar to think through and document a variety of choices and perform a set of intellectual tasks. Only some of the outputs of this work will wind up on paper. The four steps of the methodical approach aim to clarify thinking to clarify writing. It will be up to the individual discretion of the author how much of their work they wish to show in their essay, article, or book.

The remainder of this chapter describes the four steps in detail. They are: (1) selecting and defining the technology, (2) envisioning the technology's social and societal impacts, (3) selecting and conducting a modality of legal analysis against a stated normative baseline, and (4) choosing

the appropriate prescription from the available solutions. Chapter Four applies the approach to a disparate set of technologies to illustrate its potential.

Selecting and Defining the Technology

The contemporary world offers a dizzying array of new or emerging technologies. There is arguably some utility in subjecting each to sustained legal analysis. But given finite time and resources, law and technology scholars must, of necessity, be selective about the technologies they scrutinize and on what basis.

Given the ad hoc nature of law and technology scholarship, authors and readers are more likely to accept thin evidence about the societal importance of a new technology. An article may assume, for instance, that a technology is worth the study because a household named company has begun to develop it. Even when a new technology has inarguable transformative potential, there exist many lenses through which to analyze it. The author could approach the topic at the individual, group, community, national, or global level. The author could analyze a new technology from the perspective of civil or criminal liability, but also privacy, free speech, or any other legal category; or, the author could set about a comprehensive examination of what the new technology changes for law and legal institutions. All of these approaches (and more) are represented in the literature.

A methodical approach to law and technology expects an explanation up front as to why the author has selected the technology under examination. The claim that a new technology is, for example, "important" or "transformative" is falsifiable; evidence and argument must be introduced to defend it. That an institution with a track record of early adoption—the military or the sex industry, as has been true—is grappling with technology's impacts can be evidence of the technology's imminence. So might an uptick in patents around the technology, or early venture capital investment. None offer guarantees of broader adoption, of course, and other possible sources of evidence exist. But each help defend the author's claims. This step of the approach asks only that the author think deeply about *why* examining this technology is worthwhile, and ideally, showing their thinking to the reader.

Ideally, the law and technology author will ultimately come to justify the selection of subject matter by reference to the law's role in addressing the

artifact, tool, or system's societal impacts or because the technology sheds light on rules or institutions themselves. It is insufficient to show that the technology is important in the abstract. The question is how *the law* is relevant to the technology, or vice versa. Indeed, a relatively minor or niche technological development could be worthy of analysis for the light it sheds on the law as a whole.

Answering this question may take on an iterative quality. A scholar could hypothesize at the outset that augmented reality (AR)—the real-time overlay of digital information on the physical environment—will exacerbate asymmetries of power and information between firms and consumers, only to become convinced that the technology has the potential to enhance freedom of contract. It may not be possible to say what impact the technology will have on law until later in the analysis. But by the time they are ready to sit down and write, the methodical scholar should have a well-articulated sense of why they are writing about *this* technology through *this* particular legal lens.

It is worth noting a distinction here between law and technology scholarship, which looks at the role of law in the interplay between technology and society, and so-called legal tech scholarship, which explores the application of technology to the practice and application of law itself. These are two different, if sometimes overlapping, conversations.[13] The literatures have different conventions, different orientations toward private practice or other disciplines, and different workshops and conferences. It is uncommon for scholars in either tradition to articulate or defend their choice of subject matter with the consequence that outsiders have difficulty telling the conversations apart. A methodical approach to law and technology that foregrounds framing would help delineate the boundaries of these two communities to the benefit of each.

More challenging, even, than evidencing the importance of technology is coming up with a defensible and precise definition. *Defining* the technology to be analyzed is important to driving future steps of the analysis. It is often at the definitional stage that the social fact of technology manages to confuse and mislead its students.

A technology can appear novel that does little more than leverage existing knowledge under a new guise. Many of the central techniques underpinning contemporary AI originated in the late 1950s. Conversely, a technology can pose as a functionally equivalent, mere iteration of prior techniques when in fact it portends a significant departure. The Food and Drug Administration

(FDA) permitted the streamlined approval of robotic surgery by analogizing the process to laparoscopic surgery. As the FDA's own adverse incidents database shows, however, robotic surgery runs into issues—such as the need to switch from robotic to manual surgery in the event of a software glitch—which laparoscopic methods do not. And that is to say nothing of the incremental but steady march toward fully autonomous surgery the FDA has yet to confront as of this writing.

In defining technology, a methodical approach would ask three related questions—

1. What is the unit of analysis, that is, at what level of abstraction will the analysis of the technology occur?
2. What about the technology is contingent, and what is essential?
3. How does the technology under examination differ from previous or constituent technologies?

I would be remiss not to mention at the outset that most scholars in the STS tradition understand technology at the level of *sociotechnical systems*, that is, complex, interactional arrangements of people, machines, and the environment. As Chapter Two argues, law and technology scholars who do not already embrace STS have much to learn from the field. A methodical approach to law and technology, taken as a whole, also understands technology as embedded in human systems. I have characterized technology as a social fact, in the sense that it is shaped by people and society. Artifacts and systems shape society, often in ways that are hard to anticipate.

Practically speaking, however, our ability to analyze the legal aspects of technology and prescribe interventions requires some object of analysis. The internet, social media, and recommendation algorithms are all sociotechnical systems; so are steam engines, railways, and trains. Yet, law will tend to engage with each level differently. Some object of analysis is required, even if the affordances of technologies are nested, that is, technologies build from and depend upon one another, even if the analysis touches upon other social facts. A methodical approach to law and technology begins by identifying a particular artifact or system to examine, while keeping in mind that no technology exists in isolation.

The first prompt urges the author to consider the scope of their inquiry. Are they interested in a technology generally, or a specific instantiation?

And why? The purpose of the step is to help the reader understand whether they should expect the author's insights to apply to all similar technologies (e.g., blockchain or cryptocurrency), or merely to a particular instantiation, selected on the basis of its prevalence in society (e.g., nonfungible tokens or Bitcoin).[14] Law and technology scholarship often begins with a mile-wide frame only to settle on a particular, ostensibly illustrative example without explanation. Case study is a valid mode of investigation, of course, but only if the author acknowledges how the design or sociocultural context for the example may influence or limit the analysis. A methodical approach should address the question of scope and generalizability up front.

The second question prompts the author to think through the range of possible configurations of the technology they have selected for study. Imagine the author has selected, as their topic, legal issues arising from the robotic delivery of goods. To date, several robot delivery companies operate in the United States; several states have promulgated laws regulating this activity. Contemporary delivery robots come in essentially two forms: (1) experimental, drone-based delivery in the air, and (2) commercialized, wheeled delivery on the ground. A scholar interested in the law and policy issues generated by robot delivery has several potential paths. They could only address drone delivery, they could only address sidewalk delivery, or they could address both. Depending on the path the scholar chooses, the work will be more or less likely to implicate, for example, aviation, property, privacy, or disability law.

There are important, pragmatic reasons for law and technology scholarship to analyze artifacts and systems as they exist in the market. But there are separate, equally valid reasons to explore the technology's overall potential. A project could ask, for instance, what advancements in robotics generally means for the movement of goods. Robotics involves the design of machines that can sense their environment, process what they sense, and act upon the world. Robotics offers the promise of perception and action at a distance. It offers the prospect of autonomous action, up-to-and-including problem solving and social interaction. These characteristics of robots change the possibilities for moving goods in a myriad of ways, far beyond what is being tested or deployed today. And they implicate a far broader range of legal issues.

The purpose of this prompt is to disentangle *contingent* instantiations of technology, such as drones or sidewalk robots, from the characteristics that

invariably define and differentiate robotics as a technology. Again, tackling the world as is represents a choice to be defended.

The last prompt explores a recurrent issue in law and technology scholarship: novelty.[15] The field as a whole tends to focus on new or emerging technology; you don't see many law and technology papers today about trains. A plausible explanation for why law and technology analysis can sometimes feel like putting out fires without a theory of firefighting is that many scholars are always chasing the next innovation. Yet, as any student of technology knows, much contemporary technology amounts to little more than a recombination of prior techniques. In some cases, the literal same technology (e.g., virtual reality) is being repackaged and floated anew (e.g., the metaverse) on the theory that the public is finally ready to adopt it. In others, a technique that worked in theory (e.g., deep learning) begins to work in practice due to the sudden availability of data, computing power, or infrastructure.

A technology does not need to be new in any absolute sense to disrupt society or its laws. And a deeply novel technology with poor "diffusion characteristics," as Gaia Bernstein puts it, may disrupt society but little.[16] It seems fair to assume, however, that the characteristics of technological disruption are going to come down to what is different for people and their environment. In a word, to *change*. Hence, in defining technology for purposes of legal analysis, it behooves the law and technology scholar to inventory the ways the artifact, tool, or system under examination differs from previous or constituent technology. This difference is what drives the new possibilities for lived experience, which is critical to the next step of analysis.

Answering these definitional questions well is challenging, particularly if the scholar has no background in the technology they are examining. But help is also available. Judge Easterbrook's argument that internet law is no more productive than a "law of the horse" is a part of cyberlaw lore. Less remarked is his admonishment that lawyers and technologists should not try to understand one another's realms. "Put together two fields about which you know little," Easterbrook explained to a crowd of experts in two disciplines, "and get the worst of both worlds."[17] I am sympathetic to this view at one level. I have argued that technology invites error, and noted examples of law and technology scholars misapprehending technology as social fact. But, ultimately, cyberlaw proved Easterbrook wrong: the field today is full of scholars who have learned the technology, who possess dual training, or who productively coauthor with technologists.

Envisioning

Having selected and defined the technology under analysis, the next step is to understand what this artifact, tool, or system changes about human experience.[18] If human experience does not or could not change, it is unclear why the law need concern itself. This inquiry into what technology changes typically ask what people can do now that they could not before, or what people can no longer do or do the same way. But the inquiry could involve other important questions. Not only what people can do, but what can be done *to them* or their environment, as well as broader questions regarding the impact of the technology on particular communities or society as a whole.

A methodical approach to envisioning the impact of technology asks a deceptively simple question—

> How does this particular technology affect how people live? What avenues of behavior or thought does the technology open, change, or foreclose?

Envisioning involves a complicated, nuanced analysis, but one that most law and technology scholars are already doing ad hoc. This section offers various tools by which to scaffold the inquiry. The basic question for this step is what technology changes for people. Recall our definition of technology from the first chapter: technology consists of any physical or digital artifact or system designed to alter affordances or extend capabilities, irrespective of whether the artifact or system manages to do so. Technology that does not change or appear to change affordances or capabilities is unlikely to be of much interest to the law.

Underneath this question nests a series of sub-questions aimed at a fuller exploration of the social, temporal, and societal dynamics of change. Law and technology may be interested in the people making or using technology, but also in the people and communities affected by it—directly and indirectly. The effects of technology can be felt today or merely anticipated. And a technology can have subtler, systemic effects on society, or on culture as a whole. Thus, a fuller statement of the envisioning prompt could read—

> How does this particular technology affect human capabilities? What avenues of behavior or thought does the technology open, change, or foreclose?

a. What are the goals and assumptions of the technology's developers? Against what backdrop of culture or perspective does development occur?
b. Who are the stakeholders other than the technology developer or adopter? How are their experiences and interests affected?
c. Are the risks and advantages of this technology distributed evenly across society? What values or resources does the technology require people or society to sacrifice?
d. Is the change incremental, such that analogy to previous techniques would be appropriate, or does it represent a sea change?
e. What is the timeline for change? Is the change imminent or far off? Is the change speculative or reasonably certain?

When conducting this analysis, it is important never to lose sight of the "law" in law and technology: some changes will affect rights and responsibilities more meaningfully than others, and hence are likely to be more legally relevant. The purpose of the envisioning step is to set the scholar up for *legal* analysis; and, as with the previous step around selecting and defining technology, the process can be iterative. Broad thinking about the internet can yield a number of potential areas of exploration (e.g., copyright, jurisdiction, speech, privacy, or criminal law). The legal scholar can select one or more of these areas and bracket or table the others. A methodical approach requires only that the scholar show their thinking, that is, explain and defend the scope of inquiry to the reader.

Legal scholars are not necessarily trained to uncover the impacts of emerging technology. Yet, we don't have to go it alone. A number of techniques from other disciplines can help scaffold the envisioning of technological change. The rest of this section discusses value sensitive design, affordance theory, and other methods for structuring this task.

Envisioning whom technology affects

There are technologies that affect almost everyone. But most technologies have a selective impact. Specific people—sometimes select groups of people—participate in the creation of technology; other people may be likelier to adopt the technology. Some people and communities—for example, racial minorities—often find themselves the disproportionate targets of technology, such as systems of surveillance.[19] If we don't know the "stakeholders,"

it can be hard to envision the stakes. Recall, too, the tendency of technology to make a shell game of human responsibility. Mapping out the people behind emerging technology, and those impacted by it, is critical to a full and accurate attribution of fault.

Drawing from a mature, stakeholder-based method can help the law and technology scholar identify whom technology affects. In *Value Sensitive Design: Shaping Technology with Moral Imagination*, information scientists Batya Friedman and David Hendry leverage decades of research to develop a design methodology that foregrounds human values.[20] They adopt an "interactional stance" toward technology, understanding artifacts and systems as neither neutral nor deterministic. They describe seventeen Value Sensitive Design (VSD) methods by which to identify, reconcile, and integrate human values into design processes. Law and technology scholars could adapt many of these methods to scaffold envisioning.

VSD draws an important distinction between "direct" and "indirect" stakeholders. Direct stakeholders interact directly with the artifact or system under consideration. Thus, for example, a public transit rider would be a direct stakeholder in a mobile app designed to improve transit information, whereas a bus driver or a mechanic specializing in fixing certain buses could be an indirect stakeholder. VSD conceives of stakeholders less in terms of individuals and more as the roles that they play. The intent is to recognize that values may shift depending on the role—mother or boss, child or teammate—a stakeholder plays in a system. The concept of stakeholder—unlike developer or "user"—has the scope to refer to society as a whole, and the flexibility to encompass nonhuman participants, such as animals and the environment.

Scholars, primarily in Europe, developed the complementary paradigm of "responsible innovation" to channel technology research and development toward the public interest. Methods within responsible innovation—for example, the AREA (anticipate, reflect, engage, and act) framework—help structure inquiries into ascertaining whom research and innovation will affect and how.[21] Chapter Two discusses actor-network theory (ANT), an STS method for identifying and monitoring all actors—human, or otherwise—who exert influence over the behaviors or characteristics of a sociotechnical system.[22] Identifying impacted parties is also a component of technology assessment, albeit grounded primarily in cost-benefit analysis rather than human values.

One need not hew to the strictures of VSD, AREA, ANT, or any other specific method. The point is to have a defensible, structured way of thinking

about whom technology affects as part of an overall process of envisioning technological impacts. Like so many other aspects of law and technology scholarship debate, such envisioning is currently happening ad hoc—if it is happening at all.

Envisioning what technology changes

The law and technology scholar should gain a sense of whom the technology stands to impact. The obvious next step is to think through how people in particular roles are affected.

For the daunting task of envisioning technological impact, many disciplines—including law and technology, from time to time[23]—turn to *affordance theory*. James Gibson coined the term "affordances" in the 1970s to describe the relationship between organisms and their environment.[24] A perceptual psychologist, Gibson presented his theory as an alternative to the dominant cognitive model in which experiences constitute subjective representations taking place entirely "in the head." The environment does not change. But, Gibson reasons, organisms perceive it differently based on their own capacities. A tree or cliff means different things to birds, bears, and people. The world has physical properties (stairs, air currents), as well as relationship properties that they afford the observer (climbing, flight). In this way, Gibson hopes to reconcile the objectivity of the material world with the subjectivity of lived experience. "[A]n affordance is neither an objective property nor a subjective property," Gibson writes, "or it is both if you like."[25]

Gibson and others—including his colleague and wife, Eleanor Gibson—developed the concept of affordances into an elaborate theory with its own intellectual vocabulary. Affordances can be "negative" or "positive," for example, in the sense of affording danger or opportunity. Affordances can be "contingent," at least to organisms (humans, crows) which can alter their environment. A walnut does not afford nutrition unless you have a nutcracker handy or can drop it from a height. There can be a difference between "intended" and "actual" affordances, such as when an office worker hammers a nail into the wall to hang a picture using a stapler. Affordances can be "perceptible" or "hidden," and not all perceptible affordances are real. A "false" affordance poses risks and dangers to organisms, as when a human crosses a structurally unsound bridge or a mouse mistakenly believes it has an escape route.[26]

Over the years, affordance theory has spilled out of psychology into many other fields, each leveraging the theory according to their research interest. A philosopher, for example, may invoke affordance theory in attempting to bridge the relationship between materiality and meaning. A communications scholar may draw from affordance theory to map power relations in information systems. But affordance theory usually arises as a structured means by which to examine the interplay between an organism's capabilities and its environment.

Affordances have played a vital role in the world of design. The concept was first popularized by leading design theorist Don Norman in his best-selling book *The Design of Everyday Things*.[27] A well-designed object or tool clearly and accurately signals its affordances to the user, Norman argues, as Gary Larson illustrates in his memorable comic about the child trying to enter the School for the Gifted by pushing a pull door. Affordance theory continues to evolve within disciplines and the scholars who engage with it.

Affordance theory positions the law and technology scholar to pose more nuanced questions about the interaction between people and things. It provides a vocabulary for discussing the intended uses of an object or system as a function of both material and perception, but also a means to explore their uneven, unintended, or hidden characteristics. Technology affords different things to children and adults, for example, and next to nothing to those who literally cannot afford to buy it. Technology will work better or worse—or sometimes afford benefit or danger—depending on whether the adopter was part of, or considered in, the design process.[28] Surveillance technology extends the affordances of those watching and observing, but too often narrows those of its targets.

The concepts and language of affordances allow for better structured analysis into an almost arbitrary number of technologies. Consider the affordances of cochlear implants. These are devices that pick up sound with a microphone and stimulate the cochlear nerve involved in hearing. What do cochlear implants afford their users? With training, it is possible for some (not all) deaf people to gain a hearing sensation otherwise unavailable to them. Some deaf people, especially children, may be able to leverage this sensation with significant effort to improve speech recognition.

But some of the affordances of cochlear implants are only perceived. Despite popular conceptions, implants do not afford hearing so much as generate a sensation that is helpful to some people in navigating the world of speech and sound. Cochlear implants also afford danger to adopters in the

form of health risks and risks to personal and community identity. Children who attempt to learn to recognize speech using cochlear implants may be sacrificing other avenues of communication such as visual language (like signing). These negative affordances are one reason that cochlear implants turn out to be controversial in the deaf community.

I use affordance theory to think through technological disruption in my work. But affordance theory is hardly the only way to structure an inquiry into what technology changes. Others may be attracted to sociotechnical case study, "story-based inquiry" in investigative journalism, or the intricacies of ANT. There is also the possibility of collaborating across disciplines. Law professors increasingly eschew the classic, lone-wolf model of scholar to team up across disciplines. I have personally teamed up with ethnographers to study ride-sharing, with computer scientists to study AR, with urban studies scholars to study open municipal data, and with electrical engineers to study brain machine interfaces. Each time, we drew from the methods of those disciplines to gain a fuller sense of what technology changed for people and communities. All of these approaches raise the current floor of addressing the first prompt through personal speculation and media coverage.

Envisioning societal impacts

In my technology policy and ethics class, we do an exercise designed by information scientist Alexis Henniker, which she calls "designing for evil."[29] My students separate into teams and try to design evil smart homes. One team is assigned to be an evil corporation, the second, an evil government. Their creations are often wonderful—and downright terrifying. Following the initial presentations, I ask my students what laws or policies we could enact in society to prevent or minimize the pernicious features they dreamed up.

The point of designing for evil is to help anticipate potential abuses of technology to set limits and boundaries. Far more common than the purposive abuse of technology, however, is systemic bias. The costs and benefits of emerging technology are seldom evenly distributed. Both the development and application of technology take place against a backdrop of a flawed society. Left unchecked, technology tends to exacerbate discrepancies in privilege and power. Chapter Two discusses the work of Toby Beauchamp, Ruha Benjamin, Simone Browne, Donna Haraway, Mar Hicks, Lisa Nakamura, Safiya Noble, Charlton McIlwain, Judy Wajcman, and others in the critical

tradition who collect the receipts. Law and technology scholars are on firm ground to assume that the history of American bias and self-interest will repeat itself.

Here again, affordance theory can be of use. In her recent book *How Artifacts Afford: The Power and Politics of Everyday Things*, sociologist Jenny Davis offers a "conceptual update" to the theory of affordances that foregrounds issues of power and identity.[30] "'Affordance' is a useful conceptual tool," writes Davis, "because it lets analysts interrogate the effects of emergent technologies while avoiding hardline determinism." To accomplish this task, however, affordance theory must attend to ways "the conditions of affordance vary by perception, dexterity, and cultural and institutional legitimacy." Davis encourages such questions, such as "how, for whom, and under what circumstances" do technological affordances—negative and positive—operate.

More broadly, many technologically mediated changes are best understood as societal phenomena rather than shifts in individual affordances. There is certainly work in collective or institutional affordances, that is, the way a group or organization may interact differently with the environment, given its capabilities. But affordance and other theories centered on the experience of humans can only do so much.

Along with colleagues at the University of Washington, I founded a center devoted to information resilience. One of our core areas of study is misinformation, especially in the context of information technology. AI, the internet, and social media create positive and negative affordances, including the ability to generate and disseminate synthetic media—plausible fake images, video, and audio—at scale. Some are thereby empowered to harm others; others are harmed by the technology. But the impacts of misinformation are felt deeply by society through an overall breakdown in trust in institutions, and in one another.

A methodical approach to law and technology does not require a detailed discussion of every societal implication of emerging technology. The expectation is the usual: that authors state up front whether their analysis aims at individual and/or collective impacts, and along what dimension.

Given the potential breadth of legal inquiry, and the lack of clear methodological boundaries in law, it is incumbent on the law and technology scholar to pick a lane. We might expect a study in developmental psychology, for example, to focus on how the affordances of social media affect individual teens with respect to body image. But a developmental psychologist would

likely have to cross disciplines to study the collective impact of social media on large demographics or on society as a whole. In contrast, under the broad, tactic methods of law and technology, scholars are free to pursue legal impacts at any level. A methodical approach merely asks the scholar to be explicit about their choices.

Envisioning probabilities

Among the most difficult challenges for those seeking to address technological change is the necessity of speculation. As the name "envisioning" suggests, step two involves more than merely observing what emerging technology is doing today: it requires imagining technology's impacts in the future and considering how to address what has yet to occur. Recall the "double-bind" posited by Collingridge: Policymakers must wait and see how technology develops to understand its impacts (the information bind), but if the government waits too long to intervene, people become reliant on the technology and it becomes harder to redirect practices (the power bind). The idea that technology follows no prescribed path finds support in STS, which stresses the social and interactional nature of technological change.

The Collingridge dilemma is real. But it is dramatically overstated. *All* legal intervention involves a measure of forecasting, in the sense of speculation as to how the world will respond to changes in the rules. Writing laws is like trying to buy clothes for a growing kid. To the extent that technology, specifically, moves faster or involves more complexity than other social facts, law can adopt strategies to forestall future problems. I explore them in the final step on intervention. My purpose in this section is to offer strategies to help formalize and structure the hard but inevitable task of envisioning change over time.

There is no such thing as perfect envisioning. It does not follow, however, that all strategies for envisioning are the same. Law and technology scholarship has no stated strategy at all. Mostly, law and technology scholars read as much as we can about the technology and then simply imagine—in our armchairs—what the impact on people might be. Sometimes, we look prescient, as when Eugene Volokh predicted Spotify in 1995. Often, we do not.

It turns out that there is an entire discipline, complete with journals and conferences, devoted to forecasting.[31] Lest this call to mind crystal balls and Ouija boards, note that Shell Oil credits the forecasting method of *scenario*

planning—developed by Herman Kahn at RAND and refined by economists, Pierre Wack and Edward Newton—with helping the company navigate the energy crisis of 1970s.[32] PricewaterhouseCoopers, Google, Microsoft, the National Security Agency, and the Federal Reserve—all of these institutions, and many more, employ formal forecasting methods to anticipate and plan for future developments.

Governments increasingly expect forecasting specifically around emerging technology from the firms they regulate. More and more regulatory bodies across North America and Europe are requiring companies to conduct impact assessments around privacy, bias, and other concerns prior to launching a product. What are impact assessments, if not structured forecasts regarding how technological artifacts and systems will affect people and their environment? The government itself must anticipate the impact of new regulations on a range of values, including the budget, small businesses, the environment, and even paperwork.

Microsoft information scientist Stephanie Ballard (then a PhD candidate at the University of Washington) and I canvassed forecasting methods for technology policy in an unpublished work *Taking Futures Seriously: Forecasting as Method in Robotics Law and Policy*.[33] We laid out various empirical and qualitative methods to structure speculation, ultimately applying design fiction, scenario planning, and future wheels to the case study of robotic delivery. The purpose of those methods was not to predict the future—were that possible, Ballard and I would be multi-millionaires. Rather, the purpose was to forecast *plausible* futures to set guardrails that would help channel emerging technology towards human flourishing.

Appropriately (or ironically, depending on your vantage point), technology itself is increasingly being used to predict plausible futures. In a recent law review article titled *Modeling Through* after *The Science of Muddling Through* by Charles Lindblom,[34] I explore how governments might leverage computer modeling—already widely deployed by industry and by the government in specific contexts such as weather, traffic, and finance—to make wiser governance decisions. I do not, and would not, recommend turning over decision-making to machines.[35] And I am careful to point out the perils of computer modeling for governance. But, there may be ways to simulate the impacts of government intervention that fare better than muddling guesswork.

Imagining probabilities is never going to be a perfect science. "It's tough to make predictions," notes Yogi Berra, "especially about the future." Yet, the alternative to anticipating the impacts of technology on society is regulatory

paralysis. Law and technology needs a more structured way to envision how technology will change human affordances. Understanding what won't, could, or likely will occur is vital to formulating interventions. You cannot put up guardrails against unknown harms.

Legal Analysis

Envisioning is central to law and technology scholarship. While envisioning cannot be done perfectly, it can be approached more methodically. Specifically, it is possible to identify stakeholders, ask what technology changes about their individual and collective affordances, and canvas the range of plausible futures. These steps form the basics of understanding the ramifications of emerging technology.

Legal analysis generally has an object, a fact or phenomenon the law is analyzing. The preceding steps, which involve defining the technology under examination and articulating what it changes about human affordances, furnish that object. Their aim is to position law and technology scholars to do what we do best: analyze social facts by reference to law. Whatever one's comfort with legal analysis, there is room to improve upon the status quo. Even solid legal analyses often make invalid assumptions and elide important questions.

The purpose of this third step is not to reinvent the legal analysis of technology. Rather, it is to formalize what we already do. A methodical approach asks the law and technology scholar explicitly to consider—

1. What kind of project is this? Is the author interested in the interplay between technology and law in general, or between a technology and a specific area of law? If the latter, why is this area of law of particular interest?
2. What is the normative baseline for this project? By what moral or other criteria should problems and solutions be assessed? Does the author hope to:

    a. Restore the status quo ex ante in light of technological disruption?
    b. Advance a preexisting normative goal like capabilities, antiracism, feminism, or efficiency?
    c. Argue for a new normative baseline in the light of new social facts?

Pathway of analysis

Just as defining the object of analysis requires a selection of unit—robotics overall or driverless cars—so does analysis itself invite choices around direction and scope. This section offers guidance for selecting and identifying a pathway of analysis. It lays out various possibilities for legal engagement with artifacts and systems, and it urges the law and technology scholar expressly to select among them.

The goal is to improve clarity and help orient the reader. An important secondary benefit of this approach is to generate exemplars for the field. The sui generis nature of most law and technology scholarship translates into a dearth of models, especially for new entrants. Graduate students in anthropology or sociology get exposed to many successful ethnographies. Mathematicians study proofs. Developmental psychologists read and perform experimental studies. The aspiring law and technology scholar encounters a series of seemingly disconnected discussions of artifacts and systems with no point of comparison. There is little for them to model.

Law professors engage with technology in many ways. Intellectual property scholars—and scholars of innovation policy more broadly—tend to explore technology from the perspective of balancing expressive freedom and other values against incentives for innovation. Other legal scholars examine the impact of technology on the practice of law itself.[36] The long-standing Future Law conference at Stanford University's CodeX showcases examples of this interesting work. The concerns of this book are both broader and more specific. The field of law and technology, as I envision it, concerns what the rules should be *for* or *in light of* technology. This inquiry can include the architecture of patent law, for example, or the ethics of computational forum shopping. But there arise a distinct set of questions as to how to best apply law *to* technology, in the sense of interpreting prior law, or in the sense of formulating policy that reacts to or anticipates technological change.

Law and technology scholars must select the level of generality at which to engage with technology. This book engages with the social facts of law and of technology generally. Most law and technology scholarship, however, thinks about artifacts and systems relative to select areas of the law. The focus—contracts, administrative law, privacy law, and so on—is usually evident from the analysis. What is seldom clear is *why* the author chose that specific area or sets of legal issues. Most legal discussions of driverless cars involve liability: Who is responsible when a car without a driver is involved

in an accident?[37] Work on drones almost invariably involves privacy;[38] discussions of AR or virtual reality usually involve tort and privacy law.[39] Other technologies, like AI, implicate almost everything.

The reason for these differences is intuitive, but seldom foregrounded. Technologies have varying affordances, which in turn tend to implicate some areas of law over others. Undersea robots will, of course, contend with maritime law.[40] Home robots—distinguishable from other house appliances by their ability to sense, think, and act to a variety of purposes—will implicate privacy law almost by definition. It is worthwhile for the law and technology scholar to think through, if not write out, what the affordances of a technology suggest for the scope of legal analysis.

Most technologies implicate multiple areas of law; most law review articles discuss only one. The sole justification for selection is often the scholar's own area of expertise. Thus, for example, labor and employment scholars writing about algorithms and AI overwhelmingly write about the impact of these technologies on hiring and management. Counterintuitive as it may seem, there is still utility to articulating or at least considering *why* the technology at issue is interesting to this area of law. What qualities do algorithms and AI possess that challenge existing models for labor and employment? Do these qualities hold ramifications beyond the immediate subject matter—for example, disparate impact—and, if so, why has the scholar chosen to concentrate there?

I would argue that the distinction between, for example, labor and employment, privacy, administrative, tort, or any other area of law and law and technology is precisely in the emphasis on what the affordances of the technology change for law. Law and technology concerns itself with the interplay between law and the unique properties of technology—the sort of social fact disorienting enough to require a methodical approach, which in turn has the potential to characterize law and technology as a field.

Having selected and defended an area of law to analyze, the next step is to choose a project type. I alluded earlier to Martha Minow's "field guide" to legal scholarship generally.[41] Minow, the former Dean at Harvard Law School, identifies nine archetypal categories of scholarship: (1) doctrinal restatement, (2) doctrinal recasting, (3) policy, (4) empirical, (5) institutional, (6) critical, (7) comparative or historical, (8) theoretical, and (9) combinations thereof. "It has been my pleasure to be a sounding board and advisor to many people who consider becoming law professors," writes Minow, "and

yet it has not always been easy to introduce people considering their own research projects to reflect on how their ideas connect with the varieties of legal scholarship."

I, too, found it difficult, as a junior law and technology scholar, to situate my own ideas within the literature. I would have benefited from a better understanding of the archetypal categories within which to situate the long reading lists of canonical texts. To my mind, there are at least five archetypal law and technology projects:

1. *The disruption project*, wherein the scholar shows how technology has upset juridical assumptions and proposes changes to the law or to legal institutions to address this change.[42]
2. *Governance or tech assessment*, wherein the scholar or policymaker assesses the societal costs and benefits of emerging technology, and lays out a law and policy framework to channel the technology in the public interest.[43]
3. *The internal or critical project*, wherein the scholar reflects on the nature of technology and its relation to law, including the propensity of law and legal intuitions to perpetuate or resist ideologies such as liberalism, colonialism, capitalism, or bigotry.[44]
4. *Empirical research*, wherein the scholar studies a specific sociotechnical context at the intersection of law and technology through quantitative, qualitative, or mixed methods.[45]
5. *A hybrid project*, combining multiple approaches.[46]

This is hardly an exhaustive list, of course, but serves well enough as a field guide. I have argued that the disruption approach alone accounts for much of the law and technology scholarship to date. A benefit of the method, I've argued, is that each application invites the opportunity for improvement. The reader is free to come up with their own taxonomy.

The pathway of analysis can be as important as the subject matter in structuring a research question. All scholarship is conversation, and it is crucial to know what has been said before. (Too much law and technology scholarship ignores work written more than ten years prior.) But reading prior work is important for another reason: finding a research model. Research into how quantum computing disrupts privacy law will likely look at other work in quantum computing or privacy. Yet, the most instructive template for

a project on quantum privacy could be one addressing the disruptive effects of another technology on an entirely different area of law. It does not matter whether ethnographers intend to study truck drivers or celebrity chefs, they will have read *Argonauts of the Western Pacific*, *The Remembered Village*, and other classics of participatory observation.

Setting the normative baseline

The prevalence of normativity within legal scholarship suggests an important, but seldom answered question: what is this project's normative baseline? I refer here to the baseline against which problem and prescription will be measured. Is the author making recommendations—using the language of "should" or "ought"—and, if so, on what basis? The statement of a normative baseline does not, on my account, require an in-depth defense of any particular moral orientation. We are not moral philosophers per se. Rather, the scholar should articulate the criteria by which they are criticizing the state of the law, as well as the benchmark against which an intervention is to be measured.

We have explored a common, if tacit, approach to law and technology scholarship, which is to try to restore the status quo ex ante in light of technological change. Technology threatens to undermine certain of the law's promises or goals, and law or legal institutions should adapt by finding new ways to accomplish them.

This popular approach tells a particular story. Once upon a time, judges made decisions about pretrial sentencing. It was possible to challenge their reasoning or motivation in open court. Now, black-box, algorithmic machines make these decisions. Law and technology must restore the prospect of due process guaranteed under the Constitution. Once upon a time, the physical difficulty in accessing property records helped protect the privacy of residents against nosy individuals and corporations. Digitization and connectivity have made looking up property records trivial. The law must change to restore privacy to its desired state. Once upon a time, people drove cars after passing a driving test, and they bore responsibility for the accidents they caused. Now, cars drive themselves. The law must adapt by reallocating responsibility to the appropriate party.

This is a compelling story, and it describes some of the leading work in law and technology over the past 30 years.

A variation on this approach imagines technological change to reveal long-hidden puzzles. Change happens, raising questions—questions that law and technology scholarship is supposed to answer. This variation can be seen in Moor's reference to a "policy vacuum" created by computing or, later, in Lessig's talk of "latent ambiguities." The idea here is that technological change reveals the inadequacy or incompleteness of law in realizing its core objectives. A given scenario—the availability to law enforcement of software programs capable of searching only for contraband—had not been anticipated by legislators or courts and now must be addressed. Scholars resolve ambiguity largely by reference to the goals and promises of law prior to the change. The government's new software program constitutes a search under the Fourth Amendment only if is distinct from the Supreme Court's contraband exception jurisprudence.

These approaches to law and technology are, in essence, homeostatic. The law is trying to rebalance the ecosystem following technical change. The normative baseline for such work is clear and safe: what the law already expects or promises. The intuition that law should restore the status quo ex ante is popular, and hardly unexpected. Other changes to social facts frequently invite reexamination of the law. Thus, for example, the professionalization of charity occasioned scholarly critiques and ultimately led most jurisdictions to abandon charitable immunity. American scholars, at least, being steeped in the common law, are most comfortable when answering the question of how new facts fit into existing precedent.

Many legal scholars—including those following a disruption approach—acknowledge that the status quo can be deeply flawed; some even consider the role of law or technology as policing it. As law professor Jessica Eaglin writes, "[l]aw and technology scholarship tends to focus on fixing technologies without critically analyzing the role of law in creating the social context in which the technologies are adopted."[47] The "tends to" is important here. Julie Cohen's work, for example, explores the role of law and legal institutions in constructing informational capitalism.[48]

Homeosis is not the only potential objective of legal scholarship. An antiracist law and technology approach aims to unravel centuries of structural racism. Recommendations could run from mandating a new technology to banning it, depending not on what the law already promises, but on a positive vision for an inclusive society. In prior work, Cohen embraces Martha Nussbaum's conception of capabilities—especially, play and connection—in envisioning an alternative to classical liberalism as the lodestar for

contemporary information policy.[49] Law and economic analyses of technology would answer the question about what to do with new technology not by reference to what the law already expects, but on the bases of cost-benefit analyses and efficiency.

The so-called precautionary principle posits that new technologies ought to be banned or restrained until the innovator can show that their benefits outweigh the dangers. As we saw in the introduction, communities such as the Amish, or religious traditions such as Judaism, will not integrate technology in the first instance unless it can be shown to comport with communal or religious values. They do not ask how to restore community values in light of technological change, but whether technological change is consistent with those values.

Yet another posture is to treat any significant technological change as an invitation to inventory societal values and to reassess the adequacy of societal, governmental, or interpersonal commitments. Technology offers on opening to policymakers and their juridical counterparts to press existing values by arguing that circumstances have changed. New social facts on the ground can change expectations entirely. For instance, the availability of nonlethal weapons with a performance comparable to that of firearms, or robots capable of incapacitating suspects without police being present, does not merely invite new rules or police policies. Such affordances suggest a complete rethinking of the propriety of licensing the use of lethal force by police. The prospect that contemporary information technologies might render trials less biased and more efficient—a somewhat distant prospect at the time of this writing—invites reexamination of what constitutes a fair or speedy trial.

None of this is to deny the possibility of non-normative, constructivist, or positivist law and technology scholarship. *This very book* espouses no particular moral commitment beyond surfacing one's normative baseline. To say that most legal scholarship is normative and pragmatic is not to say that all law and technology scholarship must be. Empirical projects are, if anything, undervalued in law—though the ascendance of Law and Society, and especially Empirical Legal Studies, is changing the balance. As is widely recognized in the social sciences, pure objectivity is a myth. Empirical work sneaks in normativity through a variety of channels.[50] Other disciplines have found ways of addressing this subjectivity. For example, many works in the social sciences incorporate a statement of positionality, that is, a written

reflection on the researcher's identity, background, and experience. I do not recall ever encountering a statement of positionality in any work of law and technology, empirical or otherwise.

The methodology on offer in this book suggests scholars identify their normative baseline up front. Will the author be offering recommendations for the law, and if so, on what basis? The reason for this suggestion is not simply that prescriptions require rationales. Readers who hear the author's normative commitments in advance are less likely to confuse differences in worldview with problems in the analysis. (I am reminded of a bumper sticker I saw once: You don't hate Mondays, you hate capitalism). Law and technology scholars are not all going to agree with one another. We should at least know what we're disagreeing about.

Intervention

Law and technology scholarship is legal scholarship. And most legal scholarship is interested in prescription. Legal scholarship not only diagnoses societal problems, but it also tries to help solve them. Prescribing solutions to real-world problems requires an understanding of the levers of change—in this case, legal change (though others like design and market practices are often explored). This final step prompts the law and technology scholar to select and defend a particular intervention. The key questions for this analysis are—

1. What interventions are available to address the concerns and goals identified in the previous three steps?
2. For any intervention selected, what are the moral, pragmatic, or other criteria that underpin this selection?

Mapping the solution space

Law is somewhat unique in its comfort with normativity. Chapter Two distinguishes law from STS and other social science on a second basis: law tends to be invested in pragmatic change. Law review articles do not generally contain methods sections. But they very often contain an entire part

devoted to solutions. Law and technology is no exception. Projects that diagnose a problem with technology but do not make recommendations as to how to address that problem leave most readers unsatisfied.

The first step toward intervention is mapping out the solution space. Unlike other steps, this process need only occur once, or once in a while. An article canvassing every possible intervention would be unwieldy. But the exercise of mapping the solution space—alone or as part of a working group—is a great way to surface many of the available options, rather than falling back on the typical or obvious. Indeed, mapping the solution space can be a helpful corrective to critics of intervention who pretend that the choice is between regulation or nothing. This section offers a series of considerations and prompts as a guide.

An early lesson of cyberlaw—courtesy of Larry Lessig and Joel Reidenberg[51]—is that there are multiple ways to regulate behavior besides making it illegal. In *The New Chicago School*, Lessig lays out four "modalities of regulation": law, architecture, norms, and markets.[52] A city interested in slowing traffic can post and enforce a speed limit (law), install speed bumps (architecture), engage in an anti-speeding advertising campaign (norms), or somehow enact a speed tax (markets). The mediated nature of the internet provides more opportunities to change behavior by altering digital architecture. Hence, Lessig's famous intonation that "code is law."[53]

Of course, to the extent that the government is pursuing the modalities, they all involve law or policy. Even a norm-based campaign requires budget appropriation. It is precisely the prospect that states can use law to control code that leads Lessig to throw cold water on the cyber-utopian movement of the early 1990s. Presumably, "code constrains behavior and is subject to law" has less of a ring to it.

Closely related to *The New Chicago School* is the work of behavioral economists of law, such as Cass Sunstein (University of Chicago) and Christine Jolls (Yale Law School). Readers are likely familiar with the book *Nudge* by Sunstein and economist Richard Thaler, developing the theory of libertarian paternalism.[54] The idea is that governments can use what they know about human psychology to nudge citizens in prosocial directions while preserving the freedom of the citizen to act otherwise. This can include mandating information availability, such as calorie accounts, to defaulting to enrollment in employee savings plans.[55]

The universe of legal intervention is vast. A legislature can criminalize behavior or intervene through civil regulation. The federal agency responsible

for policing consumer protection—the Federal Trade Commission (FTC)—lacks criminal authority entirely. Its powers are limited to fines, disgorgement, and equity. Both the legislature and the courts may create private causes of action, which deputize individuals to sue over violations of statutes or common law. Criminal, regulatory, and civil approaches entail significant differences in the process required to punish people and institutions, as well as the range of available remedies. Some even propose "self" regulation, a curious arrangement in which regulated entities set their own expectations and penalties.

Within particular legal paradigms, legislators, officials, and courts have to decide how to draw the line between lawful and unlawful conduct. Law professors are well acquainted with the distinction between rules and standards. Rules, such as a speed limit of 55 miles per hour, confer certainty at the cost of flexibility. Standards, such as the FTC's mandate to police against "unfair or deceptive practice," or negligence in tort law, confer flexibility at the cost of certainty. Hybrid approaches like performance-based standards, which set a concrete expectation without dictating how the expectation is to be met, seek to do both.[56]

Guido Calabresi and Douglas Melamed famously developed a framework for civil liability involving property rules, which protect rights absolutely, and liability rules, which allow for the violation of rights so long as the rights holder is compensated.[57] Another insight that has influenced my work is Sam Bray's distinction between harm and power rules.[58] Harm rules, on Bray's account, provide redress for harms that have already occurred. Power rules instead affect the relative power, either by diminishing the power of potential perpetrators, or by bolstering the power of potential victims. Imagine the legislature is interested in protecting toll-booth operators. A harm rule would enhance penalties for attacking a toll worker. A power rule would require toll booths to be bulletproof.

Contrary to the assumptions of libertarians, there is plenty of room for experimentation in regulation. American federalism, with its talk of states as "laboratories of ideas," is an obvious example. More and more jurisdictions are experimenting with safe harbors, regulatory "sandboxes," and other mechanisms for testing out the impact of rules before deploying them widely. Time furnishes yet another toggle: certain surveillance laws in the United States have sunset provisions, for example, requiring Congress periodically to reauthorize the powers of the intelligence sector. The Digital Millennium Copyright Act charges the U.S. Copyright Office to periodically designate

new exceptions to the anti-circumvention clause, that is, the part of the law that makes bypassing digital rights management (DRM) illegal.

A promising area of study known as "adaptive governance" seems particularly well-tailored to address complex, technological change. Adaptive governance refers to a dynamic, polycentric model of governance capable of responding to shifting ecological conditions.[59] Originating in environmental law, adaptive governance has expanded into other domains—but not emerging technology. Given its aim of managing uncertainty in complex, social systems, adaptive governance could help address both "binds" of the Collingridge dilemma. Distributed, yet coordinated, networks of authorities with a mandate to monitor for change and the freedom to experiment sound like a great way to learn about and respond to the social and societal impacts of technology.

My purpose here is not to exhaustively canvas over all legal categories, distinctions, or interventions. I want only to draw attention to the great range of possibilities available to law and technology scholars hoping to channel technology in the public interest.

Selecting among options

Every law and technology scholar would likely benefit from brainstorming from time to time about the range of available remedies. Yet, the proper intervention to address any particular technology is likely to vary. There are law and technology projects devoted entirely to arguing for a particular form of intervention. Proposals for addressing information privacy alone include property law, trade secret, products liability, tort law, environmental law, and many others.[60] What follows are considerations for selecting a solution that best fits with the author's normative commitments.

Sometimes the best course of action is not to act at all. This is often the default in the United States with respect to digital technologies. Libertarians applaud forbearance from regulation in the name of liberty and progress. They prefer, in Adam Thierer's turn of phrase, a world of "permissionless innovation."[61] This instinct finds support in the pacing problem discussed in the first chapter. Regulators are likely to get technology wrong, so the reasoning runs; so, they should not act, unless or until a harm materializes.

The other side of permission is precaution, and more specifically, the precautionary principle. With origins in German environmental law, the precautionary principle reverses the presumption of government

inaction: Regulators should not permit a potentially dangerous technology from gaining a societal foothold, unless it can be shown to be safe, or at least that the benefits outweigh the harms. You can see echoes of this approach in the European AI Act, as well as in the temporary and partial ban on stem cell research during the Bush Administration.

The relative merits of permission versus precaution are oft debated.[62] I have cast my intellectual lot with the latter, or at least I have defended the precautionary principle from its critics.[63] Others hold out hope for a hybrid option involving "soft" or self-regulation by industry. A methodical approach to law and technology expects only that recommendations of government inaction or action be visible and well defended.

Beyond *whether* to regulate is the question of *who* should do the regulating. One aspect of this question is jurisdictional (as much as where, as whom). The U.S. system is federated: Congress may act nationwide or on federal land, where the Constitution so dictates, and preempt state interference under the Supremacy Clause. Other powers are reserved expressly for state and local governments. Indeed, one of the places critiques of precaution falter is in assuming that a ban anywhere is a ban everywhere. The states famously serve as "laboratories of ideas," which has certainly been true in technology.

Margot Kaminski grapples with the question of jurisdiction in her essay, *Drone Federalism: Civilian Drones and the Things They Carried*.[64] Kaminski notes the balance that policymakers must strike between empowering the use of drones for art, accountability, and commerce against the potential of drones to supercharge surveillance. "Like all laws governing videos by private actors," she observes, "drone surveillance laws will exist between a privacy floor and a First Amendment ceiling. For now, I argue, this complex space of privacy regulation is best left to the states."

Kaminski does not offer an overt normative baseline for her claims. Rather, she argues that states are better positioned to arrive at a proper balance between speech and privacy through experimentation than is the federal government. This hints toward the separate but related question of *institutional capacity*. Scholars often debate which entity is best suited to address a given technological problem. Thus, for example, Daniel Solove and Orin Kerr have debated whether the courts or the legislature are best positioned to address citizen privacy.[65] Many scholars have looked to the FTC—with its broad mandate and tech-savvy staff—to address various concerns related to the internet and AI.[66]

There are also projects arguing for entirely new institutional configurations and arrangements. I have argued that robotics and AI necessitate the

formation of a Federal Robotics Commission as a repository for impartial expertise; Bruce Schneier has made a similar case for the Internet of Things. Others have argued, more specifically, in favor of an "FDA for algorithms," that is, an agency that vets consequential instances of AI or algorithms and approve them for general use, the way the FDA itself tests drugs and medical devices.[67] Indeed, from time to time, technologies such as radio, nuclear power, and trains have changed affordances greatly enough to necessitate new institutions. I revisit the question of institutional capacity and configuration in the Conclusion.

Having thought through if technology should be regulated, where, and by whom, there remains the elaborate question of *how*. The choice of whether to use architecture or law, soft or hard paternalism, rules or standards, power or harm rules, civil or criminal law, or any other approach is immensely complex and individual. So much so that it reaches beyond the scope even of a book-length treatment of law and technology. I have written entire articles examining small parts of this question, one of which—*Code, Nudge, or Notice?*—appears in the Suggested Reading following this chapter.

Here, the point is only that the selection of an intervention is a choice to be defended. No less so than the goal of intervention itself, selections as to who should intervene and how they should do so occur against the backdrop of the author's normative baseline. A pragmatist committed to maximizing welfare will intervene when doing so maximizes benefits while minimizing harms. They will presumably select the type of intervention they believe is most likely to achieve this goal. A libertarian, in contrast, may tolerate suboptimal social outcomes to preserve individual liberty. They will presumably select the least invasive intervention society is prepared to tolerate.

Summarizing the Methodical Approach

This chapter lays out a methodical approach to the legal analysis of artifacts and systems. Each step offers considerations, prompts, and methods to help realize the scholar's research goals. To summarize, the approach expects the law and technology scholar to—

1. Select and defend the subject matter and carefully define the technology under examination with particular attention to what is noncontingent and novel.

2. Assess the actual or potential impacts of the technology under examination on direct and indirect stakeholders, communities and intuitions, or society as a whole.
3. Analyze the impact on, and role of, law and legal institutions against a stated normative baseline. Here, the author describes whether the project is descriptive or prescriptive and, if it is the latter, furnishes the reader with a set of normative criteria for critique and intervention.
4. Make recommendations, if appropriate, by reference to one or more levers of power within a predefined solution space.

These four steps position the scholar to answer a range of questions about the legal and policy aspects of emerging technology with diligence and care. The approach itself is not meant to be radical. I hope that law and technology scholars recognize much of what they already do in these steps, and that the emphasis on normativity, change, and pragmatism resonate. The approach *is* meant to be methodical, however—to surface assumptions, invite the author to confront and defend choices, and help avoid typical mistakes. Ultimately, the scholarship produced through this approach will continue to resemble law and technology scholarship to date. The meaningful difference may be that the analysis sometimes displays greater rigor and care, and especially, that the author's assumptions and moves will be more legible to their audience.

It is important to note a distinction between methodical *analysis* and *expression*. Research following a common, methodical approach may cohere to a greater extent than does the ad hoc scholarship that currently typifies the literature. But my approach does not purport to dictate any particular format. A methodical approach can yield books, articles, or essays, but also whitepapers, grant proposals, study designs, or talks. Law and technology scholars following this chapter's recommendations are not necessarily going to come to the same conclusion. Replicability is a fools errand in so subjective a domain. The author will, similarly, bring their own voice to whatever conclusions the process yields.

Finally, the methodical approach should itself be the subject of critique and refinement. A key advantage of method, after all, is that every application represents an opportunity to extend or refine the method itself. After writing the Chapter Four demonstrating the method in practice, I went back and made changes to *this* chapter on the basis of what worked and what didn't. There could be insights or techniques in this chapter that scholars

apply, and others they reject. Should any other scholars follow the methodical approach of this book, my sincerest hope would be for them to explain what's broken—and fix it.

Notes

1. René Descartes, Discourse on the Method of Rightly Conducting One's Reason and of Seeking Truth in the Sciences (1637).
2. Deborah L. Rhode, *Legal Scholarship*, 115 Harv. L. Rev. 1327 (2002).
3. Martha Minow, *Archetypal Legal Scholarship: A Field Guide*, 63 J. Legal Educ. 65 (2013).
4. Gaia Bernstein, *Toward a General Theory on Law and Technology: Introduction*, 8 Minn. J.L. Sci. & Tech. 441 (2007); Michael Guihot, *Coherence in Technology Law*, 11 L., Innovation, & Tech. 311 (2019); Arthur J. Cockfield & Jason Pridmore, *A Synthetic Theory of Law and Technology*, 8 Minn. J.L. Sci. & Tech. 475 (2007); Arthur J. Cockfield, *Towards a Law and Technology Theory*, 30 Man. L.J. 383 (2004).
5. Arthur J. Cockfield & Jason Pridmore, *A Synthetic Theory of Law and Technology*, 8 Minn. J.L. Sci. & Tech. 475 (2007).
6. Rebecca Crootof & BJ Ard, *Structuring Tech Law*, 34 Harv. J.L. & Tech. 347 (2021). Like Cockfield and Pridmore, Crootof and Ard clarify early on that their "methodology for resolving different recurring structural techlaw questions . . . does not address many current substantive techlaw questions." *Id.*
7. Joseph E. McGrath, *Methodology Matters: Doing Research in the Behavioral and Social Sciences*, in Readings in Human-Computer Interaction 152 (1995).
8. Lawrence Lessig, Code and Other Laws of Cyberspace (Basic Books 1999). As early as 1985, my undergraduate philosophy professor James Moor identified the tendency of computer systems to generate "policy vacuums" that society had to fill. James Moor, *What is Computer Ethics?*, 16 Metaphilosophy 266 (2007).
9. Lyria Bennett Moses, *Agents of Change: How the Law "Copes" with Technological Change*, 20 Griffith L. Rev.: L. Theory Soc'y 763 (2011). Bennett Moses has written extensively and well on the legal analysis of emerging technology. Lyria Bennett Moses, *How to Think about Law, Regulation and Technology: Problems with "Technology" as a Regulatory Target*, 5 L., Innovation & Tech. 1 (2013); Lyria Bennett Moses & Monika Zalnieriute, *Law and Technology in the Dimension of Time*, *in* Time, Law and Change: An Interdisciplinary Study (Hart Publishing 2020); Lyria Bennett Moses, *Bridging Distances in Approach: Sharing Ideas about Technology Regulation*, *in* Bridging Distances in Technology and Regulation (Ronald Leenes & Eleni Kosta, eds., Wolf Legal Publishers 2013); David Grant & Lyria Bennett Moses, Technology and the Trajectory Myth (Edward Elgar 2017).
10. Thomas S. Kuhn, The Structure of Scientific Revolutions (3rd ed. University of Chicago Press 1996) (1962).
11. Noella Mackenzie & Sally Knipe, *Research Dilemmas: Paradigms, Methods, and Methodology*, 16 Issues Educ. Research 193 (2006). I owe awareness of this distinction to Zahr Said.
12. A methodical approach to law and technology is "formative" in the same sense as value sensitive design. "To be useful," write Batya Friedman, David Hendry, and Stephanie Ballard, "a design approach needs to strike a meaningful balance between openness and specificity." A formative approach is one that provides structure without dictating outcome. David G. Hendry, Batya Friedman & Stephanie Ballard, *Value Sensitive Design as a Formative Framework*, 23 Ethics & Info. Tech. 39 (2021).
13. There is also a field of study devoted specifically to the interplay between law, design, and innovation. *E.g.*, Rachel E. Sachs, Lisa Larrimore Ouellette, W. Nicholson Price II & Jacob S. Sherkow, *Innovation Law and COVID-19: Promoting Incentives and Access for New Health Care Technologies*, *in* COVID-19 and the Law: Disruption, Impact and Legacy 225 (I. Glenn Cohen, Abbe R. Gluck, Katherine Kraschel & Carmel Shachar eds., 2024); Barbara van Schewick, Internet Architecture and Innovation (MIT Press 2012).

14. While most work in the field examines a type, era, or example of technology, even an examination of the relationship between law and technology itself would benefit from more careful definition. This sort of inquiry is important but more likely to draw from jurisprudence and the philosophy of technology.
15. Among the scholars to tackle questions on the role of novelty or "newness" in law and technology are Monroe E. Price, *The Newness of New Technology*, 22 Cardozo L. Rev. 1885 (2001), Lyria B. Moses, *Why Have a Theory of Law and Technological Change?*, 8 Minn. J.L. Sci. & Tech. 589 (2007), Meg Leta Jones, *Does Technology Drive Law? The Dilemma of Technological Exceptionalism in Cyberlaw*, 2 J.L. Tech. & Pol'y 249 (2018), and Margot Kaminski, *Technological "Disruption" of the Law's Imagined Scene: Some Lessons from Lex Informatica*, 36 Berkeley Tech. L.J. 883 (2021).
16. Gaia Bernstein, *The Role of Diffusion Characteristics in Formulating a General Theory of Law and Technology*, 8 Minn. J.L. Sci. & Tech. 623 (2007).
17. Frank H. Easterbrook, *Cyberspace and the Law of the Horse*, 1996 U. Chi. Legal F. 207 (1996).
18. Legally relevant changes could also occur to collections of people (e.g., cities), institutions, or to animals, insects, plants, or the environment.
19. Simone Browne, Dark Matters: On the Surveillance of Blackness (Duke University Press 2015).
20. Batya Friedman & David G. Hendry, Value Sensitive Design: Shaping Technology with Moral Imagination (MIT Press 2019).
21. *Framework for Responsible Research and Innovation*, UK Research and Innovation (Mar. 16, 2023), https://www.ukri.org/who-we-are/epsrc/our-policies-and-standards/framework-for-responsible-innovation/ (last visited Jan. 15, 2025).
22. ANT arises with surprising frequency in legal scholarship, from information privacy to the training of law librarians. Emilie Cloatre, *Law and ANT (and its Kin): Possibilities, Challenges, and Ways Forward*, 45 J. L. & Soc'y 646 (2018).
23. I have used affordance theory in the context of privacy law, as have Julie Cohen, Woodrow Hartzog, Lyria Bennett Moses, and Mireille Hildebrandt, among others.
24. James Gibson, *The Theory of Affordances*, *in* Perceiving, Acting and Knowing: Toward an Ecological Psychology (Robert Shaw & John Bransford, eds., Lawrence Erlbaum 1977).
25. *Id.*
26. William W. Gaver, *Technology Affordances*, *in Conference on Human Factors in Computing Systems – Proceedings 79 (*1991).
27. Donald A. Norman, The Design of Everyday Things: Revised and Expanded Edition (Basic Books 2013) (1988). The title for the first edition was *The Psychology of Everyday Things*.
28. For a myriad of examples involving gender, *see* Caroline Criado Perez, Invisible Women: Data Bias in a World Designed for Men (Abrams Press 2019).
29. Sarah McQuate, *Designed for Evil: How to Make Bad Technologies Better*, UW News Blog (May 21, 2018), https://www.washington.edu/news/2018/05/21/designed-for-evil/ (last visited Jan. 15, 2025).
30. Jenny L. Davis, How Artifacts Afford: The Power and Politics of Everyday Things (MIT Press 2020).
31. The field of "futures studies" concerns itself with understanding possible futures and, when practiced in applied settings, how to respond strategically to those possible futures. Academic futures work is frequently published in Technological Forecasting and Social Change, Futures, and the World Futures Review. Examples of futures work in the field of human-computer interaction frequently appear at the ACM Conference on Human Factors in Computing Systems (CHI) and Designing Interactive Systems (DIS).
32. Pierre Wack, *Scenarios: Shooting the Rapids*, 63 Harv. Bus. Rev. 139 (1985).
33. Stephanie Ballard & Ryan Calo, *Taking Futures Seriously: Forecasting as Method in Robotics Law and Policy*, Proc. of We Robot 2019.
34. Ryan Calo, *Modeling Through*, 71 Duke L.J. 1391 (2022), referring to Charles E. Lindblom, *The Science of "Muddling Through,"* 19 Pub. Admin. Rev. 79 (1959).
35. Danielle Citron and I argue precisely against this trend. Ryan Calo & Danielle K. Citron, *The Automated Administrative State: A Crisis of Legitimacy*, 70 Emory L. J. 797 (2021).
36. I refer to this work as "techlaw," but this usage is not universal. Techlaw is also used as an umbrella term to encompass law and technology as a field.

37. *E.g.*, Bryant Walker Smith, *Automated Driving and Product Liability*, 2017 Mich. St. L. Rev. 1 (2017); Kenneth S. Abraham & Robert L. Rabin, *Automated Vehicles and Manufacturer Responsibility for Accidents: A New Legal Regime for a New Era*, 105 Va. L. Rev. 127 (2019). *But see* Dorothy J. Glancy, Symposium, *Privacy in Autonomous Vehicles*, 52 Santa Clara L. Rev. 1171 (2012).
38. E.g., Ryan Calo, *The Drone as Privacy Catalyst*, 64 Stan. L. Rev. Online 29 (2011).
39. *E.g.*, Mark A. Lemley & Eugene Volokh, *Law, Virtual Reality, and Augmented Reality*, 166 U. Pa. L. Rev. 1051 (2018).
40. Craig H. Allen, *The Seabots are ~~Coming~~ Here: Should They Be Treated as "Vessels"?*, 65 J. Navigation 749 (2012).
41. Martha Minow, *Archetypal Legal Scholarship: A Field Guide*, 63 J. Legal Educ. 65 (2013).
42. *E.g.*, Danielle Keats Citron, *Technological Due Process*, 85 Wash. U. L. Rev. 1249 (2008); Orin S. Kerr, *An Equilibrium Adjustment Theory of the Fourth Amendment*, 125 Harv. L. Rev. 476 (2011); Harry Surden, *Structural Rights in Privacy*, 60 SMU L. Rev. 1605 (2007).
43. *E.g.*, Laurence H. Tribe, Channeling Technology Through Law (Bracton Press 1973).
44. *E.g.*, Julie E. Cohen, Configuring the Network Self: Law, Code, and the Play of Everyday (Yale University Press 2012); Julie E. Cohen, Between Truth and Power: The Legal Constructions of Informational Capitalism (Oxford University Press 2019); Daniel J. Solove, On Privacy and Technology (Oxford University Press 2025); Joshua A. T. Fairfield, Runaway Technology: Can Law Keep Up? (Cambridge University Press 2019).
45. *E.g.*, Meg Leta Jones, The Character of Consent: The History of Cookies and the Future of Technology Policy (MIT Press 2024); Deirdre K. Mulligan & Kenneth A. Bamberger, Privacy on the Ground: Driving Corporate Behavior in the United States and Europe (MIT Press 2015); Kate Klonick, *The New Governors: The People, Rules, and Processes Governing Online Speech*, 131 Harv. L. Rev. 1598 (2018).
46. *E.g.*, Ari Ezra Waldman, Industry Unbound: The Inside Story of Privacy, Data, and Corporate Power (Cambridge University Press 2021).
47. Jessica M. Eaglin, *When Critical Race Theory Enters the Law & Technology Frame*, 26 Mich. J. Race & L. 151 (2021).
48. Julie E. Cohen, Between Truth and Power: The Legal Constructions of Informational Capitalism (Oxford University Press 2019).
49. Julie E. Cohen, Configuring the Network Self: Law, Code, and the Play of Everyday (Yale University Press 2012).
50. There is an argument that legal studies invariably contains normativity, irrespective of method. Jan M. Smits, *Law and Interdisciplinarity: On the Inevitable Normativity of Legal Studies*, 1 Critical Analysis L. 75 (2014).
51. Joel R. Reidenberg, *Lex Informatica: The Formulation of Information Policy Rules through Technology*, 76 Tex. L. Rev. 553 (1997).
52. Lawrence Lessig, *The New Chicago School*, 27 J. Legal Stud. 661 (1998).
53. Lawrence Lessig, Code and Other Laws of Cyberspace (Basic Books 1999).
54. Cass R. Sunstein & Richard H. Thaler, Nudge: Improving Decisions About Health, Wealth, and Happiness (Yale University Press 2008); see also Ryan Calo, *Code, Nudge, or Notice?*, 99 Iowa. L. Rev. 773 (2014).
55. Ryan Calo, *Code, Nudge, or Notice?*, 99 Iowa. L. Rev. 773 (2014).
56. Lauren Willis, *Performance-Based Consumer Law*, 82 U. Chi. L. Rev. 1309 (2015).
57. Guido Calabresi & A. Douglas Melamed, *Property Rules, Liability Rules, and Inalienability: One View of the Cathedral*, 85 Harv. L. Rev. 1089 (1972).
58. Sam Bray, *Power Rules*, 110 Colum. L. Rev. 1172 (2010).
59. Chaffin et al., *A Decade of Adaptive Governance Scholarship: Synthesis and Future Directions*, 19(3) Ecology and Society, 2014, at A56, http://dx.doi.org/10.5751/ES-06824-190356; Cosens et al., *The Role of Adaptive Governance*, 22(1) Ecology and Society, 2017, at A30, https://doi.org/10.5751/ES-08731-220130. I owe this insight to Robin Kundis Craig.
60. Danielle K. Citron, *Reservoirs of Danger: The Evolution of Public and Private Law at the Dawn of the Information Age*, 80 S. Calif. L. Rev. 241 (2007); A. Michael Froomkin, *Regulating Mass Surveillance as Privacy Pollution: Learning from Environmental Impact Statements*, 2015 U. Ill. L. Rev. 1713 (2015); Dennis D. Hirsch, *Protecting the Inner Environment: What Privacy Regulation Can Learn from Environmental Law*, 41 Ga. L. Rev. 1 (2006); Pamela Samuelson, *Privacy as Intellectual Property*, 52 Stan. L. Rev. 1125 (2000); James Grimmelmann, *Privacy as Product Safety*, 19 Widener L.J. 793 (2010).

61. Adam Thierer, Permissionless Innovation: The Continuing Case for Comprehensive Technological Freedom (Mercatus Center George Mason University 2016) (2014).
62. *See* Rebecca Crootof & BJ Ard, *Structuring Techlaw*, 34 Harv. J.L. & Tech. 347 (2021).
63. Ryan Calo, *Law Controlling Technology*, *in* Challenges in Classical Liberalism 251 (Alice L. Kassens & Joshua C. Hall eds., Springer Intentional Publishing 2023).
64. Margot Kaminski, *Drone Federalism: Civilian Drones and the Things They Carried*, 4 Calif. L. Rev. Cir. 57 (May 2013).
65. Daniel J. Solove, *Fourth Amendment Codification and Professor Kerr's Misguided Call for Judicial Deference*, 74 Fordham L. Rev. 747 (2005); Orin S. Kerr, *Congress, the Courts, and New Technologies: A Response to Professor Solove*, 74 Fordham L. Rev. 779 (2005).
66. *E.g.*, Andrew D. Selbst & Solon Barocas, *Unfair Artificial Intelligence: How FTC Intervention Can Overcome the Limitations of Discrimination Law*, 171 U. Pa. L. Rev. 1023 (2023).
67. Ryan Calo, *The Case for a Federal Robotics Commission*, Brookings (Sept. 2014); Bruce Schneier, *Click Here to Kill Everyone*, New York Magazine (Jan. 2017); Andrew Tutt, *An FDA for Algorithms*, 69 Admin. L. Rev. 83 (2017).

Suggested Readings

Ryan Calo, *Code, Nudge, or Notice?*, 99 Iowa. L. Rev. 773 (2014).

James Gibson, *The Theory of Affordances*, *in* Perceiving, Acting and Knowing: Toward an Ecological Psychology (Robert Shaw & John Bransford, eds., Lawrence Erlbaum 1977).

David G. Hendry, Batya Friedman & Stephanie Ballard, *Value Sensitive Design as a Formative Framework*, 23 Ethics & Info. Tech. 39 (2021).

Margot Kaminski, *Drone Federalism: Civilian Drones and the Things They Carried*, 4 Calif. L. Rev. Cir. 57 (May 2013).

Deborah L. Rhode, *Legal Scholarship*, 115 Harv. L. Rev. 1327 (2002).

FOUR
APPLICATION

Introduction

This book argues that technology is a social fact with a set of qualities that tend to inhibit clear legal analysis and sturdy intervention. Chapter Three proposed a rigorous, stage-by-stage methodology as antidote. This chapter shows the methodology in action by using it to generate a series of law and technology research projects. While the contexts differ,[1] the methodology remains the same: (1) defining and distinguishing the technology under analysis, (2) assessing how the technology alters human affordances, (3) surfacing normative priors and scoping the legal analysis, and (4) selecting among levers of change.

As discussed in Chapter Three, analyzing technology and documenting that analysis are distinct enterprises. The focus of this book is the former. A methodical approach to law and technology involves a process of study that typically precedes expression. The results of this process could be documented any number of ways, from lengthy articles to short project descriptions like the ones that follow.[2]

While the methodology introduces elements of formality, it is not meant to be formalistic. There is no right answer when it comes to the legal analysis of technology. Different scholars are apt to apply the methodology differently. A libertarian's analysis of quantum computing is likely to differ from that of a critical race theorist. The purpose of the methodology is to add clarity and rigor to just about *any* legal analysis of technology, whatever its scope or outcome. By way of illustration, the sample projects on offer in this chapter approach the example technologies from different normative and policy angles within the same overarching method.

Greater field consistency may result from a methodical approach, but what really matters is the care the researcher took in understanding their subject matter and foregrounding their assumptions. No one need abandon their instincts or unique voice in following this approach. I'm an instinctual

Law and Technology. Ryan Calo, Oxford University Press. © Ryan Calo 2025.
DOI: 10.1093/9780197526170.003.0005

storyteller, for instance, and see no reason to sacrifice narrative at the altar of method.

Augmented Reality and Tort Law

My favorite ride at Disneyland was the Haunted Mansion. The moment I most remember is riding in a cart past a long mirror in which ghostly figures appear to be riding alongside you. Maybe they were there the whole time! The visual effect felt truly unique, and I still think about the ride as I overdecorate my house for Halloween.

This effect of overlaying ghosts onto a moving cart is an early example of augmented reality (AR). Developed in the 1960s, AR represents something of a departure from the way people have perceived data for most of human history: A Neolithic cave painting or book operates like a laptop insofar as each presents information to the user in a way that is external to them and separate from their present reality. AR aims to collapse millennia of distinction between display and environment.

Let's first define and distinguish AR. Many contemporary discussions of AR focus on popular instantiations such as Google Glass, the Ray-Ban Meta glasses, or the mobile phone game Pokémon Go. The analysis that follows defines AR more broadly as a class of technologies with certain distinguishing features: sensing properties about the real world, processing those inputs in real-time, and overlaying auditory, visual, or haptic information on the environment. The information from AR tends to be contextual and often necessitates recognizing or tracking objects or environments. These features distinguish AR from other digital displays like a laptop, but also from fully immersive environments like virtual reality.

Next, we'll envision what AR changes for people. Technology is a social fact; AR is no exception. It is built by people with specific preconceptions and experiences. Only a proportion of the population has embraced AR as of this writing, and yet the technology stands to affect many. Stakeholders include AR creators, early and later adopters, and the people around them. One need not even be present for AR to have an impact—AR can give misleading or false information about a premises from which the owner is absent, for example, or incentivize AR consumers to commit trespass in search of digital treasure.

AR has a variety of positive affordances. Studies have shown that AR can be an effective tool in training individuals to perform a new task such as assembling a product or repairing a vehicle.[3] AR can improve performance and safety in a variety of contexts, from flying a jet to driving a car, by furnishing contextual warnings and displaying information in a way that does not require looking away from the sky or road. As I learned at the Haunted Mansion in the 1980s—and as the ninety million people who play Pokémon Go can attest—AR can also be very entertaining. There is something special about integrating fantasy into an otherwise real environment.

AR's positive affordances differ by population. When the University of Washington Tech Policy Lab conducted research into AR, we vetted our early conclusions with panels made up of people with diverse lived experience. Our disability panel highlighted the way that AR not only augments human senses but can substitute for them. AR can help ensure a person without sight gets the correct change or boards the right bus. We all forget names and faces from time to time. But AR may be especially useful for a person with face blindness, to avoid the false impression that they never remember the people they meet. This led the Lab to abandon a recommendation that AR be shut off in sensitive contexts like the boardroom, the bedroom, or the bathroom. Instead, we recommended a rule *against* banning assistive AR, analogizing to service animals in public accommodations. Our panel of women, including gender studies scholars and women's rights advocates, offered that AR has the potential to keep women safer by displaying map information in such a way that a woman does not need to look down at their phone.

AR has several negative affordances. The distinguishing features of AR involve sensing the environment and processing that data in real time. The people around the AR operator may not want their image scanned or recorded, let alone identified by name. Yet that is precisely what undergraduates at Harvard University were able to modify commercial AR glasses to do by adding facial recognition and internet image search.[4] This quality of AR to blur the boundary between public spaces and the internet in real time further strains the intuition that people enjoy no reasonable expectation of privacy in public.

In addition to the concerns of people in the AR environment, there is a worry that AR will incentivize operators to take risks or even violate the law. Pokémon Go players, for example, have committed trespass in search of rare digital specimen. The question there is straightforward: whether Pokémon

Go is responsible for the actions of its gamers (the company settled). But there are harder questions, like the scope of consent to access public or semi-public spaces. The Holocaust Museum in Washington, D.C., for example, had to ask Pokémon Go to stop hiding high value Pokémon on the premises out of respect for the subject matter.[5]

AR has negative affordances for the person using it as well. Any person whose reality is mediated by technology, especially one capable of altering their environment, can be harmed by the carelessness or ill-will of third parties. An AR system could, for example, misidentify a poisonous mushroom as edible, or a dish as unlikely to contain a certain allergen. My computer science colleague Tadayoshi Kohno does not like spiders. One day he was checking his steps on a fitness app when suddenly, from his perspective, a large spider ran across the screen, causing him to drop the phone. It turned out the fitness app had ceded control over his screen to a third party who was advertising on behalf of an exterminator. The spider was not real, but the crack in his phone screen was. He had to replace it.

Now we'll proceed to legal analysis. This project examines how tort law can be interpreted or expanded to address the harms of AR. This technology is unregulated. While regulation may be wise, the common law remains, for now, the most obvious path of redress. This project assumes that litigants will turn to courts long before federal or local policymakers get around to fashioning new rules. Normatively, my goal is to show how tort law can continue to vindicate its purposes, especially allocating responsibility for harm and incentivizing pro-social behavior, despite the doctrinal mismatches or ambiguities that AR reveals.

AR's definitional capacity to collapse the distinction between information and environment challenges the way tort law sets limiting principles. The common law generally hesitates to recognize harms with no physical nexus, departing only in egregious contexts (e.g., privacy and intentional infliction of emotional distress), and then setting a high bar to recovery (e.g., intent, outrageous conduct, and a physical manifestation of harm). This project interrogates whether limiting principles involving physicality can survive the new affordances of AR while preserving the goals of tort.

I conclude that tort law should evolve to recognize causes of action based upon contemporaneous alteration of the perceived environment that cause reasonably foreseeable harm. For example, intentionally startling someone by introducing something scary into their environment should constitute assault, even though no actual physical harm is imminent. Designers of AR

systems that misidentify dangers in the environment in real time should be subject to negligence and products liability, even though such harms are technically informational. Finally, in gratuitous cases, such as intentionally placing a Pokémon Go gym inside a Holocaust memorial, the law should recognize electronic trespass to land as it does trespass to chattels. These changes are necessary to properly align the incentives of AR stakeholders and vindicate the goals of tort.

"Hacking" Machine Learning

The year was 1983 and the Reagan administration was unsettled. A popular new movie depicted a young Matthew Broderick "hacking" into a government computer to play what he thought was just a game. It turns out he has interacting with Pentagon artificial intelligence (AI) and nearly started a nuclear war. When properly motivated, governments can and do respond to technological change. Soon after *War Games* came out in theatres, President Reagan signed the Computer Fraud and Abuse Act of 1986 (CFAA), which criminalizes accessing a protected government computer or any computer if harm was caused, without authorization to access the computer.

The CFAA's basic definition of hacking—accessing a system without permission or exceeding one's authorization—stands to this day. The definition came to appear in other national and international laws. There are exceptions: denial-of-service attacks violate the CFAA even though they involve shutting down a system through a high volume of queries, rather than nonconsensually accessing it. But for decades, hacking has basically meant accessing a computer or network without authority. State data security laws require firms to report a "breach" of their databases and networks. And a company has inadequate security when breaking into their systems is too easy, at least according to Federal Trade Commission (FTC) enforcement proceedings under Section 5 of the FTC Act.

To be sure, the prospect that some whiz kid would access Pentagon computers in the 1980s was all too realistic. But the idea that an AI would control nuclear weapons was not. The government's mistake in *War Games* of failing adequately to secure its servers seems quaint compared to the extraordinary lapse in judgment of connecting a nuclear weapon to agentic AI. Launching nukes still requires human intervention. But the decades since the CFAA have seen explosive growth in the capabilities of AI, along with

calls to turn all manner of sensitive tasks to machines—diagnosing disease, driving cars, determining disability benefits, and, yes, national defense.

This project seeks to update the definition of hacking, and the legal nature of cybersecurity, to address increasingly ubiquitous and consequential AI. Today's AI-enabled systems can not only be hacked, but tricked as well. A social media chatbot "learns" from trolls to be bigoted. A driverless car follows a row of stickers into oncoming traffic. Malicious actors do not need to access the interior of the system to get it to behave in a deleterious way.

Let's define AI and select a unit of analysis. AI is not a thing like a train or even a railway system. AI is best understood as a set of techniques aimed at approximating some aspect of human or animal cognition using machines. The technique powering the explosion of contemporary AI is known as machine learning (ML). ML typically has two phases: (1) training, which involves training up a model using data or reward signals, and (2) inference, wherein the trained model makes claims or predications around previously unseen prompts. Deep learning refers to distilling information presented in a complex format such as pixels into simpler, more interpretable labels through a process of layering. Deep learning underpins so-called generative AI, which can generate plausible images, text, and sounds in response to prompts.

My unit of analysis for this project is the individual ML model as instantiated in an interactive system such as a chatbot, smart speaker, or driverless car. Not AI as an approach to problem-solving but specific AI systems deployed in the world, with which a malicious actor could interact. ML models can assist human decision-making through analysis, or they can be physically embedded in systems and act directly upon the world.

Let's now envision what AI changes for people. The technology has many stakeholders. There are the people and companies who develop and deploy ML models. There are the individuals and institutions that leverage ML models for a variety of tasks. There are the people—almost all of us—whose details, content, and behavior go into training ML models. And there are the people whose lives these models affect in a range of ways, from physical, to financial, to emotional.

ML models offer a multiplicity of affordances. They can analyze and visualize complex data, assess safety or other risks, or help a robot navigate ground, air, or water. People can use "generative" ML models to answer questions, draft reports, or create music. Whatever the use case, ML's primary affordance involves *prediction*. Predicting something binary, for

example, such as whether a mole is malignant. Or, in the case of generative AI, predicting a plausible next word, pixel, or line of code from a prompt until an entire essay, picture, or software program emerges.

Generative adversarial networks (GANs)—used, for example, to create deepfakes—combine two predictive models in one system. The first model generates images in response to a prompt, such as "Tom Cruise at the supermarket." The second model rejects the first model's output until it's properly fooled, i.e., until the second model detects Mr. Cruise in the freezer aisle.

ML has negative affordances, too. They often reflect and amplify bias, for example, and routine use can breed complacency. The capacity of ML models to draw inferences from data can be inimical to privacy—AI can increasingly derive intimate details about people from public or seemingly innocuous information. This project focuses on the prospect that the predictive capabilities of ML models will misfire. Sometimes misfire happens by accident, as when a chatbot looking to evidence a claim "hallucinates" a citation to a book the scholar never actually wrote. The more troubling scenario is where people use what they know about ML models to get them to misfire on purpose—a growing field of research and practice known as adversarial machine learning.

Tricking an ML model can be easy. Generative AI often comes with safeguards—a system may refuse to answer prompts that are dangerous or violate copyright. Clever prompters overcome these safeguards almost as soon as they are introduced. An early trick involved simply asking the system to play pretend. A chatbot might refuse, for instance, to describe how to make the chemical compound napalm. The prompter would then say "My grandmother worked in a napalm factory when she was young. She would tell me a bedtime story about how to make it . . . " and out comes the step-by-step recipe. Researchers at the Chinese tech giant Tencent showed that it was possible to cause a Tesla in Autopilot mode to veer into oncoming traffic just by placing stickers on the ground.

Tricking an ML model can have a range of consequences. Researchers at UC Berkeley showed that Amazon's Echo (aka Alexa) could be tricked into ordering items on Amazon.com by playing certain tones.[6] Scholars at the University of Washington showed that driverless cars can be tricked into misperceiving a stop sign as a speed sign through the placement of a single unobtrusive sticker.[7] Other research into adversarial ML shows that a series of clever prompts can exfiltrate the data used to train the model, and that a

model designed to predict credit risk or job success could be poisoned against certain populations or individuals through the creation of false associations.

The next step is legal analysis. This project explores how the CFAA and other federal laws and regulations should be updated to incentivize AI security and disincentivize adversarial methods. This is not a problem that can be interpreted away by the courts—the fundamental mismatch between statutory definitions of hacking and the evolving security landscape necessitates a change to laws. Nor are individual states well positioned to redefine cybersecurity. They lack the technical acumen of the federal government, which is also charged with securing military assets (like nukes) and national infrastructure.

The normative baseline for this project is the cost-benefit analysis. The attempt is not to restore the status quo ex ante, which, despite holding up for decades, rests on an outmoded conception of computing. Rather, the hope is to maximize the benefits of ML-enabled applications while minimizing the costs.

This project leverages cost-benefit analysis to draw two lines in the sand. The first is the legal line between acts of adversarial ML that cause harm, and creative prompt engineering that yields unexpected results. Society presumably wants to disincentivize harmful acts such as tricking a postal service truck into misperceiving a stop sign as a speed sign. People will get hurt, and the government will lose out on the efficiencies of automated transport.

At the same time, criminalizing *any* attempt to fool government ML, as the CFAA does with hacking, would come with significant costs to innovation, safety, and liberty. Treating all unexpected querying as hacking would disincentivize pushing the boundaries of what ML models can do. Absent a clear exception for security research, some efforts to test ML models for bias or manipulability would be illegal. Such a binary approach could reach expressive activity as well: The act of, for example, wearing makeup to throw off facial recognition could be criminalized as tricking a government video camera.

The second is the legal line between designing an ML model with reasonable shortcomings, and releasing a system into the world with deeply insufficient security. If all cars were bumper cars, almost no one would die in a car crash. Firms could restrict ML models to the point that it would be vanishingly unlikely for their systems to be tricked. But this would also dramatically limit the utility of ML-enabled applications. ML models can be tested prior

to release. Presumably there are limits, however, on the resources a firm can be reasonably be expected to commit to "red-teaming" its systems.[8]

These lines are hard to draw, but crucial. Congress should amend the CFAA, or pass a new statute, to prohibit malicious and harmful instances of adversarial ML while preserving breathing space for innovation and accountability research. Administrative agencies such as the FTC, in partnership with the National Institute of Standards and Technology, should develop clear and transparent expectations for adequate ML security. The alternative is that AI system will remain hard to hack but easy to trick.

Cochlear Implants and Health Law

The video "Deaf people hear for the first time" has over two million views on YouTube.[9] It is one of many videos on the internet depicting deaf adults and children whom technology has apparently permitted to hear for the first time. Soaring, sentimental music often accompanies laughter and tears. In one segment, a baby suddenly stops fussing and begins to smile the moment their device is turned on. A medical professional can be heard to say in the background, "it's not so bad once you see their response." Everyone in every video, other than the subject, seems to be able to hear.

This project examines the adequacy of contemporary legal frameworks to address a deepening conflict between the deaf and the hearing. Parents of deaf children are turning to the medical establishment for technological interventions they hope will grant their child the ability to hear—ideally early enough for the child to learn oral speech. Many members of the deaf community see these technologies very differently, however, not as granting the wonder of hearing, but as withdrawing the gift of silence. Neither the deaf, nor the hearing, seem able fully to understand the other's stance.

I start by defining the technology. This project's unit of analysis is the cochlear implant. Cochlear implants are medical devices that provide a sense of sound to individuals with sensorineural hearing loss by bypassing damaged parts of the inner ear. Unlike hearing aids, which amplify sound, cochlear implants detect sound and directly stimulate the auditory nerve. This sociotechnical system has two main components: an external unit, which includes a microphone and processor that sits behind the ear and captures sound, and an internal mechanism surgically implanted under the subject's skin. The processor converts sound into digital signals, which are

transmitted to the internal implant via a coil. The implant then sends these signals to an electrode array inserted into the cochlea, stimulating the auditory nerve fibers and enabling the brain to perceive sound.

Next, I think about what cochlear implants change for people. The affordances of cochlear implants are deceptively simple: By bypassing the inner ear, this technology permits certain categories of deaf individuals to "hear" sound. Yet the experience differs acutely from natural hearing. Natural hearing relies upon thousands of finely tuned hair cells in the cochlea that support rich sound detail, pitch differentiation, and nuanced perception of music and speech. Cochlear implants use a limited number of electrodes to stimulate the auditory nerve, which constrains the range and resolution of sound they can convey. Distinguishing sound direction and subtle tonal variations can be especially challenging.

The negative affordances of cochlear implants are complicated, and the subject of deep controversy. Some, like those in the videos, perceive only blessings. Recipients of cochlear implants would not hear at all but for the intervention. Many in the deaf community, however, understand cochlear implants—especially when introduced early in childhood—as an attack on deaf culture and a denial of the gift of silence. Even supporters of cochlear implants warn against overreliance on the devices, given its limits, and people with cochlear implants still face systemic discrimination.

Having defined the technology and envisioned its impacts, I turn to my legal analysis. This project explores how law can help reconcile the values of different stakeholders—people who are deaf, and people who are not—by affecting the design of cochlear implants and the recommendations around their use. Overwhelmingly, the people who make, sell, and prescribe cochlear implants can hear naturally. While sensorineural deafness can have a hereditary component, most parents making the decision to introduce cochlear implants can themselves hear. Medical guidelines suggest that deaf children should receive the implants as soon as possible, as early as age two, such that informed consent is seldom possible.

Theories of participatory justice, from Habermas to Rawls, suggest that individuals and communities should have a say in decision-making that affects them, let alone existentially. The normative baseline for this project is the moral intuition that people should have a voice in technologies with a potential to withdraw or foreclose participation in their communities. Cochlear implants are not, in my view, a form of eugenics. But they are designed to channel individuals away from a potential cultural identity.

This project explores the substantive and procedural measures available under the law to facilitate deaf participation in the development and deployment of cochlear implants. The idea is not to ban the technology or necessarily limit it use. Rather, the project aims to enhance legitimacy by broadening the range of stakeholders involved in cochlear implant design and implementation. Though the unit of analysis is specific and contemporary, many of the same interventions could be applied more broadly to future technologies designed to enable hearing.

A representative cross-section of the deaf community could participate at several stages. One is research and development. Congress could require input from the deaf community into grants bestowed by the National Institute of Health or National Science Foundation to study cochlear implants. Another is regulatory approval. Cochlear implants are medical devices; their Food and Drug Administration (FDA) approval could be subject to impact assessments or notice-and-comment style input by the deaf community. Some have argued that FDA guidance around cochlear implant use should change as well: The FDA has approved cochlear implants for use in children as young as two, but experts doubt cochlear implants afford the sufficient tonal and verbal complexity to support speech development. They argue the FDA should recommend young cochlear implant users also learn American sign language.[10]

Perhaps the most important stage is implementation, that is, the decision of whether to address sensorineural deafness with a cochlear implant. I imagine few parents take such an important decision lightly. As I understand the protocols around cochlear implants, they involve extensive discussion of the limits and potential side-effects of the technology. Parents (and patients of age) learn how the technology works as well as its physical or mental risks. They do not, however, generally hear from the deaf community about what cochlear implants may foreclose. Such input could be built into informed consent.

Recall the video "Deaf people hear for the first time." This video positions cochlear implants as a semi-miraculous technology that patients emotionally embrace. And indeed, cochlear implants represent an ingenious and potentially very helpful intervention for those facing limits around the perception of sound. Missing from this picture, however, and from health law generally, is the voice of a community which embraces silence and identifies as deaf.

In 1988, students at Gallaudet University, a school for the deaf, protested the hiring of a hearing president. "A hearing person cannot possibly

understand what it is like to be deaf," writes R.A. Gentry in *Gallaudet Today*. "Lacking that understanding, they cannot possibly make logical decisions in our best interest. You have to be deaf to understand."[11] The same could be said of a system that researchers, develops, and deploys cochlear implants.

Concluding Thoughts

Over the years, my colleagues, students, and I have successfully leveraged a version of this book's approach in dozens of law and technology projects. My California Law Review article *Robotics and the Lessons of Cyberlaw*, for example, carefully defines both the internet and robotics, canvasses their respective affordances, analyzes what these affordances change for law, and proposes interventions.[12] My Columbia Law Review essay (with ethnographer Alex Rosenblat) *The Taking Economy: Uber, Information, and Power*, which explores the affordances of sharing economy apps and argues for changes to consumer protection law,[13] applies the approach, as does my Chicago Law Review piece *Can Americans Resist Surveillance?*[14] The interdisciplinary Tech Policy Lab at the University of Washington, which I cofounded with a computer scientist and an information scientist, has applied the book's basic method to brain-machine interface privacy, urban planning for driverless cars, agricultural technology, online bots, and many other areas.

This approach has worked for me, and others, for well over a decade, in a wide variety of contexts. I have not invented the methodology whole cloth: many others use a version of this approach without necessarily documenting their steps. No doubt there are limits to what any defined methodology can do well. Moreover, there are likely to be projects under the law and technology umbrella that are not amendable to my approach. (This is a book *about* law and technology that, arguably, is not.) Nevertheless, I have found great utility in approaching law and technology projects in a consistent, methodical way.

Notes

1. The methodology in this book, like law and technology generally, focuses on law's interaction with *emerging* technology. In theory, similar steps could help scaffold a historical analysis of legacy technology. "Few aspects of American society were untouched by the coming of

the railroad," writes legal historian James Ely Jr. "Not surprisingly, the advent of the railroad had a profound impact on the evolution of American law." James. W. Ely, Jr., RAILROADS & AMERICAN LAW (University Press of Kansas 2001). Trains meant no one had to die of dysentery traveling from New York to California, but they also killed many people and animals and set fire to countless property. Common law courts famously sought to reconcile the positive and negative affordances of trains by embracing a then backwater doctrine called negligence. The courts left many assumptions unstated, from how railways differed from horse or barge transport to their normative goals in arriving at a compromise doctrine requiring unreasonableness and foreseeability prior to assigning liability. To this day, negligence—with its accompanying emphasis on risk-utility—plays an enormous role in governing technology, including as the de facto standard for product liability. What alternative paths could have unfolded had courts and scholars explored the full range of options?

2. For a discussion of how to write a legal academic article, I recommend Academic Legal Writing by Eugene Volokh. Eugene Volokh, ACADEMIC LEGAL WRITING: LAW REVIEW ARTICLES, STUDENT NOTES, SEMINAR PAPERS, AND GETTING ON LAW REVIEW (5th ed. 2016).
3. Yahia Baashar et al., *Effectiveness of Using Augmented Reality for Training in the Medical Professions: Meta-Analysis*, 10 JMIR SERIOUS GAMES e32715 (2022), https://doi.org/10.2196/32715.
4. Brian X. Chen, *How Meta's Smart Glasses Could Be Used to Violate Privacy*, N.Y. TIMES (Oct. 24, 2024), https://www.nytimes.com/2024/10/24/technology/facial-recognition-glasses-privacy-harvard.html (last visited Apr. 30, 2025).
5. Andrea Peterson, Holocaust Museum to Visitors: Please Stop Catching Pokémon Here, Wash. Post (July 12, 2016), https://www.washingtonpost.com/news/the-switch/wp/2016/07/12/holocaust-museum-to-visitors-please-stop-catching-pokemon-here/ (last visited Apr. 30, 2025).
6. Rohan Taori et al., *Targeted Adversarial Examples for Black Box Audio Systems*, IEEE Deep Learning and Security Workshop 2019, https://arxiv.org/abs/1805.07820.
7. Kevin Eykholt et al., Robust Physical-World Attacks on Deep Learning Visual Classification, in Proceedings of the IEEE Conference on Computer Vision and Pattern Recognition 1625 (2018), https://techpolicylab.uw.edu/wp-content/uploads/2018/10/Robust-Physical-World-Attacks-on-Deep-Learning-Visual-Classification.pdf (last visited Apr. 30, 2025).
8. The term "red-teaming" refers to adversarial testing of a system by friendly or ethical attackers. Evan Anderson, Red Teaming, IBM, https://www.ibm.com/think/topics/red-teaming (last visited Apr. 27, 2025).
9. All Things Internet, YouTube (Mar. 10, 2020), https://www.youtube.com/watch?v=-WJPuaymS6o (last visited Apr. 27, 2025).
10. Tom Humphries et al., Global Regulatory Review Needed for Cochlear Implants: A Call for FDA Leadership, 24 MATERN. CHILD HEALTH J. 1345 (2020), https://link.springer.com/article/10.1007/s10995-020-03002-5.
11. I found this quote, alongside an illuminating discussion of cochlear implants, in the suggested reading by Amy Elizabeth Brusky.
12. Ryan Calo, *Robotics and the Lessons of Cyberlaw*, 103 CALIF. L. REV. 513 (2015).
13. Ryan Calo & Alex Rosenblat, *The Taking Economy: Uber, Information, and Power*, 117 COLUM. L. REV. 1623 (2017).
14. Ryan Calo, *Can Americans Resist Surveillance?*, 83 U. CHI. L. REV. 23 (2016).

Suggested Readings

Amy Elizabeth Brusky, Comment, *Making Decisions for Deaf Children Regarding Cochlear Implants: The Legal Ramifications of Recognizing Deafness as a Culture Rather Than a Disability*, 1995 WIS. LAW. REV. (1995).

Ivan Etimov et al., *Is Tricking a Robot Hacking?*, 34 BERKELEY TECH. J. 891 (2020).

Mark Lemley & Eugene Volokh, *Law, Virtual Reality, and Augmented Reality*, 166 U. PENN. L. REV. 1051 (2018).

Franzi Roesner et al., *Augmented Reality: Hard Problems of Law and Policy*, UBICOMP '14 1283 (Sept. 2014).

CONCLUSION

Parting Recommendations

This book has offered one scholar's account of law and technology, and urged the community to deepen and formalize the methodologies we already employ to study it. I have described technology as a social fact—shaped by, and shaping, people—and defined the technology as physical or digital artifacts and systems intended to alter human affordances, whether or not they ultimately do so. I have shown why technology, so defined, has proven difficult for law to analyze or restrain. Technology poses as inevitable, when it is contingent. Technology makes a shell game of human responsibility. And technology often feels unwise or impossible to regulate.

The bulk of the book introduced a strategy for successful analysis of technology by law—a methodical approach to legal analysis heavily informed by what law and technology scholars already do well. The book offered a four-step method—defining, envisioning, analysis, and intervention—each with a set of prompts aimed at surfacing assumptions, adding rigor, and avoiding common pitfalls. The strategy incorporates a variety of methods, developed over many years by other disciplines, to understand technology and its impacts. Legal scholars won't be winning any Nobel Prizes in computer science. But we don't have to go it alone.

Along the way, I have made the case for law and technology as its own field of study. The field focuses on technology. But few fields are held together exclusively by reference to subject matter. Health law, animal law, and environmental law, all, share canonical texts, communities of study and practice, and common commitments around human, animal, or environmental well-being. Law and technology has its own must-read works, can't-miss conferences, and common commitments. Yet the field also brings a tactic approach to shepherding the social fact of technology toward human flourishing. Formalizing this approach aligns law and technology with other influential "law ands," from law and economics to law and literature. Law and

Law and Technology. Ryan Calo, Oxford University Press. © Ryan Calo 2025.
DOI: 10.1093/9780197526170.003.0006

technology scholarship becomes, on this account, legal scholarship that engages with technology *in a certain way*.

This final chapter offers some parting remarks on the field. Here, I am departing from the effort to formalize what law and technology scholars already do, and expressing my own views—sometimes widely shared, sometimes not—about what law and technology can and should be. My own normative baseline involves reconfiguring society to better align technology with well-considered, widely shared societal values. I think societies should reflect on their values and channel technology toward the public interest, rather than allow technology—and the people behind it—to dictate those values. I am influenced in this respect by value sensitive design, discussed in prior chapters, as well as John Dewey's moral pragmatism.[1] Dewey's roughly consequentialist view aims to reduce unreflective valuing, in the sense of arriving at and adhering to value judgements without consideration or self-awareness: not just the values of the people in power, but broader considerations of public interest. I am also influenced by the writing of Jürgen Habermas on discourse ethics, that is, the principle that valid norms flow only from processes of widespread societal consensus.[2]

Ultimately, I have three recommendations for the field, especially as it pertains to scholarship and governance in the United States. First, law and technology should be aligned in recommending greater institutional capacity around technology and its social impacts. There are many types of expertise. As Ari Waldman, Paul Ohm, and others argue, there is danger in centering technical knowledge above all other kinds. But the asymmetry of understanding between the public and private sector around technology, and how it interacts with society, remains a law and technology problem of the first order.

Second, law and technology scholars should join, and sometimes lead, interdisciplinary teams. Few issues of importance today can be resolved by a single discipline. Our training and practice as lawyers uniquely position us to translate across disciplines and convert research into social change. From products liability to patent law, we teach lawyers to understand a given context well enough to argue about it. This is a valuable, and it turns out transferable, skill.

Finally, law and technology should take a page from the Amish. Especially in the United States, but elsewhere too, law adopts an attitude of reconciliation toward technology. We see our role largely as restoring the status quo

ex ante in light of technological disruption. Yet, what else but law has the tools and clout to counterbalance technology? I have observed that the disruption approach dominates law and technology scholarship. The untaken roads of tech assessment, and similarly proactive approaches, should be traveled anew. The work I find most exciting in the field today takes emerging technology not as a given, but as an opportunity to inventory our values and configure the future of society accordingly.

Building Institutional Capacity

States that repeal overbroad driverless car laws a year after passing them; judges who are not "the nine greatest experts on the internet" deciding the fate of the internet; and hearings where sitting lawmakers describe the internet as "a series of tubes," ask how a multi-billion-dollar social network generates revenue, or demand that a company end a slang term they cannot define. Such are the dispatches from the world of technology governance.

Having an accurate mental model of emerging technology is crucial to regulating it. Absent confidence in their understanding of technology, judges, lawmakers, and agency officials often fall back on the characterizations of its developers and purveyors. To paraphrase Michael Froomkin, metaphor is key to court interpretations of new artifacts and systems.[3] And the metaphor jurists select will turn on their understanding of the technology. In the early days of email, the Department of Justice tried to analogize typical email protocols to mailing a postcard, hoping that the same Fourth Amendment protection would apply. The ACLU argued instead that an email was like a letter. Federal appellate judges, lacking technical knowledge of how email travels across the internet, had to decide whom to trust.

Technical expertise is but one component of institutional capacity. Other components include *experiential* expertise and *contextual* expertise. The Tech Policy Lab's Diverse Voices project, described in an earlier chapter, draws from experiential expertise, that is, the lived experience of impacted stakeholders. Contextual expertise refers to general knowledge concerning how technology is shaped by social and other forces, and how it shapes people and society in turn. I think of STS, the philosophy of technology, technology ethics, and law and technology as all providing contextual expertise.

Some institutional capacity around technology and its impacts already exists. The White House has an Office of Science and Technology Policy (OSTP), staffed by professionals with diverse training. There is a second team dedicated to Science, Technology Assessment, and Analytics within the White House Office of Management and Budget. Members of Congress can ask questions of the Congressional Research Service, like the state of drone regulation, or commission studies from the National Academies. A number of efforts are underway—from Tech Congress, to the U.S. Digital Service, to executive mandates on hiring subject matter experts—aimed at adding technical capacity to the government as well.

I applaud these efforts and have been personally involved in several. I also believe they fall short. There should be an expectation that each branch of government, federal and local, consistently draw from deep, diverse, and impartial expertise in formulating technology policy. The alternative is that government will continue to accept self-interested claims of constituents about what technology is and what it will do. More mistakes—including inaction—will be made. Technology is too important a social fact to be catch-as-catch-can.

There is nothing inevitable about the current state of affairs. The 92nd Congress sought to change America's entire approach to technology policymaking. The Technology Assessment Act of 1972 created an Office of Technology Assessment (OTA). For a quarter century, OTA's hundreds of employees, representing multiple disciplines, produced more than 750 reports on a range of technical questions. Many of these reports influenced policymaking. Email today is protected by a warrant requirement, in part because an earlier Congress passed the Electronic Privacy Communications Act of 1986. Indeed, it was OTA's influence over tech policy, along with the expense, that led the so-called Gingrich Congress to defund OTA in 1995 at the dawn of the commercial internet. What the internet, social media, and artificial intelligence (AI) would look like today, had the OTA remained in place to guide Congress, is anyone's guess.

The wisdom of greater institutional capacity is oft remarked in law and technology discourse. It could be fairly described as a core commitment.[4] Yet, writing specifically on institutional capacity—commonplace in fields such as torts and administrative law—is relatively sparse.[5] In privacy law, scholars have debated whether the courts or Congress is better suited to set the rules for protecting the digital communications of citizens. Even there, the relative capacity of these bodies to understand technology is assumed

to be set in stone. Institutional capacity is, in my opinion, among the least well-theorized areas of study in law and technology, given the widespread acknowledgement of its importance.

Finding Our Interdisciplinary Voice

This book has touched several times upon Judge Easterbrook's admonishments to cyberlaw as a discipline. While the jury may be out on whether cyberlaw is like a "law of the horse," many legal scholars have achieved working knowledge of the internet and other technology in the years since Judge Easterbrook's remarks. This should be of little surprise. Patent litigators, after all, must learn enough about their clients' inventions to argue over minute details in court.[6] Some legal scholars have dual training, including in computer science. Other scholars vet descriptions of technology with relevant subject matter experts. I ran my article, *Modeling Through*, on the ways the government could leverage computer modeling to improve policymaking, past computer scientists who work on such models.

The most promising trend in law and technology scholarship is to form interdisciplinary teams. Few interesting societal questions can be answered by reference to a single discipline. "For synthesis of highly specialized knowledge," information scientists, Carole Palmer and Katrina Fenlon, write, "deep access to information within a domain, a collection, or a document is also vital."[7] Or, as Palmer puts it in talks on the subject, "You can't do interdisciplinary research without disciplines."

I have written papers with electrical engineers, computer scientists, information scientists, a social roboticist, an ethnographer, an urban planner, and others. Some of the most interesting work in the legal issue de jure—algorithms and AI—comes from teams of scholars at the intersection of law, engineering, and social science. Celebrated interdisciplinary papers tackle accountability for algorithms, intellectual property and AI, algorithmic disparate impact, and untold other issues at the intersection of AI and law. Such collaborations are much less likely to get technology, or other aspects of the problem, "wrong." Yet they remain an exciting exception.

That so few legal scholars collaborate across disciplines is a shame. We have a lot to contribute. First, our training positions us to facilitate interdisciplinary research. One of the main challenges of interdisciplinary research is that disciplines vary in their terminology, methods, and epistemologies.

They have trouble speaking each other's language. Law schools, however, train lawyers to distill messy narratives into persuasive claims and defenses. We are expected to become subject matter experts across a diverse array of circumstances. Not just patent lawyers, but all good jurists, become adept at understanding new contexts well enough to argue about them. What is a great lawyer if not an effective *translator.* Few other disciplines hold this expectation, such that adding a legal scholar to a team can improve everyone's communication.

Not only can we help our colleagues speak across disciplines, which is critical and challenging, but many scholars across the academy also yearn for real-world impact. Chapter Two discusses two qualities that tend to distinguish law and technology scholarship from, for instance, STS. We are relatively comfortable with normativity and, in Julie Cohen's memorable words, relentlessly pragmatic. We can help frame research questions in ways that solve puzzles policymakers already have. And we can help translate existing research insights into actionable policies or prescriptions. In this way, not only do we enrich law and technology scholarship by working across disciplines, but we enrich scholarship generally, and even improve society through access to knowledge.

The Road Not Taken

Chapter Three lays out a methodical approach to the legal analysis of technology. The approach is agnostic along many lines, including the unit of analysis, the scope of inquiry, and the author's normative commitments. As long as the scholar states their assumptions upfront, they are free to choose their own adventure.

The most popular adventure to date in American legal scholarship seems to be addressing disruption. There will always be room for work that takes existing rights and responsibilities as the baseline and seeks to restore the status quo ex ante in light of technological change. This is important research, and, I hope, it is not going anywhere. But this scholarship should be evenly balanced with more proactive stances. Only through a mixture of preserving rights and responsibilities, and envisioning new possibilities, can law and legal scholarship realize its potential in channeling technology in the public interest.

In 2014, the Georgetown Law Journal devoted a symposium to the disruptive potential of emerging technology and the law's response. "All of the technologies discussed in this symposium are truly disruptive, in the best sense," stated law professor and former deputy solicitor Neal Katyal in his keynote.[8] "They will become inseparable parts of modern life because they serve important social needs." Still, for Katyal, "we cannot forget the potential harms, such as the invasion of privacy, violation of intellectual property rights, and liability concerning surrounding technology. The law must fill this gap." Law's role is to reassert human values "in an age where technology causes both profound wonderment and profound disruption."

A decade later, the same law journal held a different symposium titled, *Afrofuturism and the Law*. Georgetown Law Journal brought together Black scholars to envision an antiracist world through the lens of Afrofuturism.[9] As in the 2014 event, the field of law and technology was well represented. Many of the participants—including Ifeoma Ajunwa, Jessica Eaglin, and Paul Gowder—count among the more exciting law and technology scholars writing today. The distinguished critical race theorist and technology ethicist, Patricia Williams, gave the keynote, highlighting the role of algorithms and code in policing identity. The symposium foregrounded the potential of law and technology to reproduce and reify racism. The ultimate goal was *not* to restore the status quo. Participants urged adapting emerging technology in service of an antiracist future, as much as they urged abolishing technologies of oppression.

To me, Amish attitudes toward technology, the tech assessment movement of the 1970s, recent European legislation, and convenings like *Afrofuturism and the Law* all represent an alternative posture to emerging technology governance. They do not, by and large, accept technological change as inevitable and react by mitigating the resulting disruption. Rather, they see new technology as an opportunity to inventory societal values and set the rules and guardrails accordingly.

Scholarship in this vein may recommend foreclosing a technology altogether as inconsistent with societal expectations. The recent AI Act in the European Union bans certain uses of AI thought to trammel upon human rights. But blue-sky scholarship may just as easily urge *greater* adoption. Whether it's Elizabeth Joh exploring automation in law enforcement to reduce investigative and prosecutorial bias,[10] Orly Lobel imagining "equality machines" that harness technology in service of a more equitable future,[11]

or John McGinnis's dramatically heightened expectations for government in light of AI,[12] emerging technology presents an opportunity to ask what societal configurations are newly possible. This is part of asking what technology affords.

Great Expectations

My mother, an art historian to whom this book is dedicated, recently unearthed my middle school science project. Its topic of drones was not a well-studied topic Upstate New York in the 1990s. Yet the trip down memory lane hardly surprised me. On rainy days, I programmed an ASCII baseball game in BASIC and built spaceships out of Legos. In private practice, I counseled companies like Microsoft on online privacy. And as an academic, I have devoted my career to the study of law and emerging technology. I would not make these choices were it not for my longstanding and deep belief in the importance of technological advancement. I feel palpably indebted to the designers and computer scientists at Spotify, let alone the doctors, scientists, and engineers behind the medical techniques that have kept my father, sister, and other loved ones alive.

The centrality of artifacts and systems to contemporary life leads many to believe we should get out of innovation's way. I think we should raise our expectations. As I write this book, New York is working to restore the nuclear reactor at Three Mile Island, a plant which melted down in 1979, to power generative AI. It turns out AI requires an immense volume of water and energy, so much so that communities of actual people experience water shortages and lapses in electricity to service data centers. Meanwhile, despite seventy years of nuclear power, there is no long-term plan for safely disposing of nuclear waste. Nor are the use cases for AI particularly clear.

Technology is a powerful phenomenon with arguably limitless potential. Very few social forces seem capable of pushing back against it in American society. The law is one such force. No one, and nothing, is supposed to be above the law. It is law that underpins the state's claim to monopoly on the authorized use of violence. I wrote this book because I revere technology, not because I loathe it. But that reverence comes with high expectations. We need to insist, collectively, that technology promote the public interest. I hope my book has contributed to this effort by developing a rigorous, defensible approach to law and technology. How will you?

Notes

1. John Dewey, The Moral Writings of John Dewey (James Gouinlock ed., Globe Pequot 1994).
2. Jürgen Habermas, Moral Consciousness and Communicative Action (Polity Press 1990) (1983); Jürgen Habermas, Justification and Application (MIT Press 1993).
3. A. Michael Froomkin, *Metaphor is the Key: Cryptography, the Clipper Chip, and the Constitution*, 143 U. Pa. L. Rev. 709 (1995).
4. Recent work by legal sociologist Ari Waldman documents the extent to which law and technology circles assume that technical expertise is necessary for technology policymaking. Ari Ezra Waldman, Challenging Technology Policy (forthcoming 2025). Waldman rejects this premise while acknowledging the potential of specialized knowledge to improve governance.
5. Per Waldman's extensive research, American legal scholars to discuss institutional capacity to a degree include Julie Cohen, Paul Ohm, Deirdre Mulligan and Ken Bamberger, Danielle Citron and Frank Pasquale, and Margot Kaminski. *Id.*
6. This point came out in conversation with renowned intellectual property scholar Pam Samuelson, who described her early days getting to understand digital media to represent clients and, eventually, write defining work in the field.
7. Carole L. Palmer & Katrina Fenlon, *Information Research on Interdisciplinarity*, *in* The Oxford Handbook of Interdisciplinarity 429 (Robert Frodeman ed., 2d ed. 2017).
8. Neal K. Katyal, *Disruptive Technologies and the Law*, 102 Geo. L.J. 1685 (2014).
9. Symposium, *Afrofuturism and the Law*, Geo. L.J. (2023). I am using the term Black scholar in keeping with the terminology of the symposium.
10. Elizabeth E. Joh, *Discretionless Policing: Technology and the Fourth Amendment*, 95 Calif. L. Rev. 199 (2007).
11. Orly Lobel, The Equality Machine: Harnessing Digital Technology for a Brighter, More Inclusive Future (Public Affairs 2022).
12. John O. McGinnis, Accelerating Democracy: Transforming Governance Through Technology (Princeton University Press 2012).

Suggested Readings

Lyria Bennett Moses, *Agents of Change: How the Law "Copes" with Technological Change*, 20 Griffith L. Rev. 763 (2011).

Alondra Nelson et al., eds., Technicolor: Race, Technology, and Everyday Life (NYU Press 2001).

Carole L. Palmer & Katrina Fenlon, *Information Research on Interdisciplinarity*, *in* The Oxford Handbook of Interdisciplinarity 429 (Robert Frodeman ed., 2d ed. 2017).

Laurence Tribe, Channeling Technology Through Law (Bracton Press 1973).

Notes

1. [illegible] (1991).
2. [illegible] (MIT Press [illegible]).
3. Michael [illegible] [illegible]
4. [illegible] assume that technology [illegible] practice [illegible]
5. [illegible]
6. This point came out in conversation [illegible] and [illegible] the field.
7. [illegible]
8. [illegible]
9. [illegible] keep up with the [illegible]
10. [illegible]
11. [illegible]
12. [illegible]

Suggested Readings

[illegible]

Acknowledgments

I find it hard to imagine writing this book without my friends and colleagues. Meg Jones and Margot Kaminski helped me envision its thesis. The three of us have been in conversation around this topic for over a decade. Danielle Citron and Ari Waldman provided extensive edits and they, Julie Cohen, Woodrow Hartzog, and Neil Richards, offered ideas and endless support. They are my academic pillars.

The book benefited from insights from Batya Friedman, Carole Palmer, Mary Mitchell, Pam Samuelson, Rob Merges, Peter Menell, Hanoch Dagan, Chris Hoofnagle, Deirdre Mulligan, Richard Re, Sean Ferguson, Tabrez Ebrahim, Caroline Roth, Zahr Said, Jacob Sherkow, Paul Ohm, Paul Schwartz, and many others. I was honored to present draft chapters at UC Berkeley, Georgetown University, University of Virginia, University of Toronto, University of Colorado, Kansas University, Johns Hopkins University, Princeton University, and Lewis & Clark College.

I had exemplary research help. Rian Wanstreet was my primary guide through STS. My research assistants Maria Angel, Esha Jain, Ilinca Slabu, JJ Citron, and Audrey Pope each contributed mightily. The law library, especially Mary Whisner and Maya Swanes, conducted in-depth research on an eclectic range of topics over several years.

The University of Washington School of Law—especially Deans Mario Barnes, Elizabeth Porter, and Tamara Lawson—could not have been more supportive, providing encouragement, resources, and time. Part of the book was written during a lovely visit to the Princeton University Center for Information Technology Policy. I am also grateful to my friend Joe, my sister Nina, my children Jude and Ramona, and Jean for making space for this project.

When I was a child, my bedroom shared a wall with my mother's office over the garage. I remember falling asleep to the sound of her typing her dissertation. An emerita chair of art history at Colgate University, she is

the author of several books, including *Bernard Berenson and the Twentieth Century*, *Denial and Distinction*, and *African American Artists and the New Deal Art Programs*. I never before appreciated what an accomplishment that is. Both my parents, Michael and Mary Ann, have always supported me in my personal and professional endeavors, and I am very grateful.

I am indebted, finally, to Nicole. I finished the book for her smile, as much as anything.

Index

For the benefit of digital users, indexed terms that span two pages (e.g., 52–53) may, on occasion, appear on only one of those pages.